Joe DiMaggio

The Yankee Clipper

Published by: Beckett Publications
15850 Dallas Parkway
Dallas, TX 75248

Manufactured in the United States of America

ISBN: 1-887432-60-4

Cover photo by National Baseball Library
and Archive / Cooperstown, N.Y.

Second Edition: October 1998

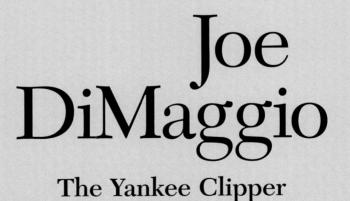

Joe DiMaggio

The Yankee Clipper

By the staff of Beckett Publications

A Legend for All Times

Joe DiMaggio's standard of excellence
has endured through time, eliciting the faith
of three generations of baseball fans

If only we could turn back time.

The early 1930s may not have been the best of times for most Americans amid the Great Depression. But out West, baseball fans were watching a young star develop in the Pacific Coast League.

The star's name was Joseph Paul DiMaggio.

He debuted with the San Francisco Seals as a fill-in at shortstop and shortly thereafter made a name for himself with a 61-game hitting streak. Turning back time would allow us to witness the making of a legend.

In 1936, DiMaggio took his show to the grand stage of Yankee Stadium. It was there where he reignited the Yankees' winning tradition, leading New York to World Series titles in each of his first four seasons.

DiMaggio may have best been known for his phenomenal hitting prowess, as evidenced by his trademark 56-game hitting streak in 1941. His speed and quickness in the field also allowed him to adequately cover the large amount of outfield real estate in Yankee Stadium.

But Joe has become more than just a great athlete from the past. Even today, more than 45 years after his retirement, Joe represents a symbol of pride for Americans.

For those who have dreamed of witnessing Joe DiMaggio at his best, it isn't necessary to turn back the clocks. We at Beckett Publications have assembled a grand compilation of fantastic photos and stories detailing the career and modern-day aura of the great Yankee Clipper himself — Joe DiMaggio. Enjoy!

Mike Pagel

Mike Pagel
Associate Editor

Beyond his status as a legendary Yankee, Joe DiMaggio has evolved into an American icon.

UPI / BETTMANN

Contents

American Royalty

One of baseball's greatest players ever,
Joe DiMaggio also has become one of
the nation's most revered living legends

For almost 60 years, he's been a part of the American consciousness.

Ever since Joe DiMaggio burst onto the Major League Baseball scene like a meteor in 1936 with the New York Yankees, he has developed a presence acclaimed in song, venerated by adoring fans and respected in virtually all walks of life.

Still active beyond his 83rd birthday, Joe blesses baseball functions throughout the country with his presence when he's not spending quiet and relaxing retirement days in the South Florida sunshine.

At Yankee Stadium in 1995, dressed in his trademark blue suit, white shirt, floral tie and black shoes, DiMaggio threw out the ceremonial first pitch on Opening Day and drew a long standing ovation from a sellout crowd.

The legend of his persona has been passed down from father to son, so that even today's generation — ballplayers and fans alike — regards him highly. Voted "the greatest living player" in 1969, he carries that mantle with obvious pride and dignity.

"Mrs. Robinson," the Simon and Garfunkel song written years after Joe's retirement and carrying the memorable line "Where have you gone Joe DiMaggio?" brought him back into the national limelight. Other lyrics

By George De Gregorio

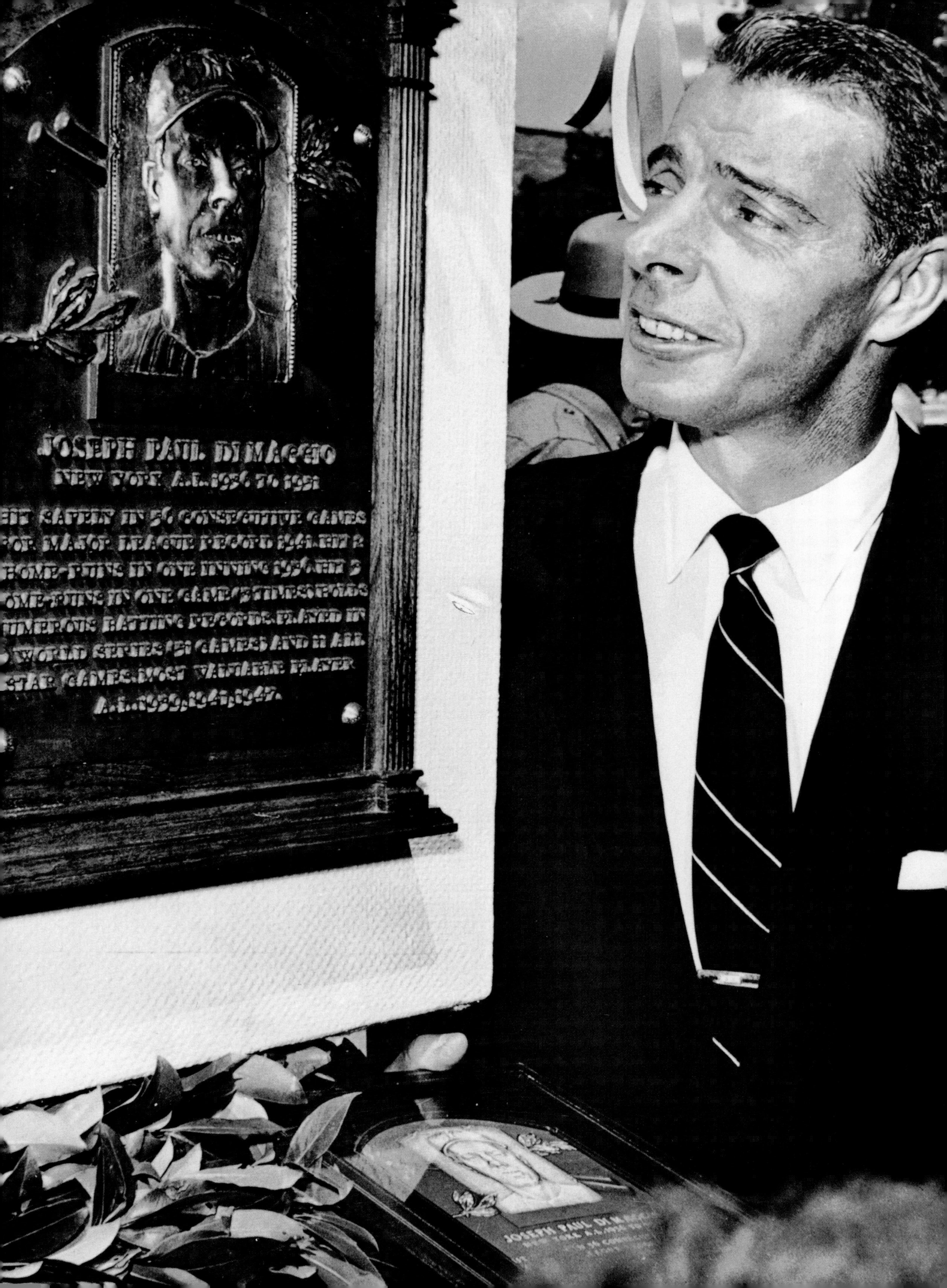
JOSEPH PAUL DI MAGGIO
NEW YORK A.L. 1936 TO 1951

extolled his virtues as a ballplayer, too. For example, "her skin is as tender as DiMaggio's glove" was penned by Oscar Hammerstein for South Pacific, as a tribute to DiMaggio's flawless style as a center fielder.

A quiet man, who protected his privacy and rarely indulged in media interviews, DiMaggio has been obliging in a genial way in his later years. Although he has adamantly refused to write a slick autobiography, he still maintains a pleasant rapport with the press. He willingly gives an autograph and is sought out by young and old fans alike.

After playing 13 seasons, he retired in 1951. DiMaggio's television ads for Mr. Coffee and his work as a spokesman for the Bowery Savings Bank in New York kept his image alive for the public. He became an avid golfer, but in recent years after a pacemaker implant, his chief exercise has been walking. His much-publicized marriage to Marilyn Monroe, their divorce, and his subsequent touching role at her funeral made him at once both a tragic and heroic public figure. His first marriage, to Dorothy Arnold, also an actress, produced their son, Joe Jr., and ended in divorce.

In his heyday, his baseball talents rated second to none. In San Francisco, where he broke in with the Seals of the Pacific Coast League, he became a legend, hitting in 61 consecutive games, and even then seemed a sure bet to reach the majors. The DiMaggio name was easily recognizable in San Francisco. His brothers, Dom and Vince, were outstanding ballplayers who also enjoyed careers in the major leagues.

When Joe joined the Yankees in 1936, the team had not won a pennant since 1932. He was an instant success: a .323 batting average, 29 home runs and 125 RBI. The Yankees romped to the pennant by 19-1/2 games and then beat the New York Giants in six games in the World Series. DiMaggio had a tremendous series. The rookie batted .346, with nine hits, three RBI and three runs scored.

Whether sharing a laugh with Ted Williams or spending a special moment with his son, Joe Jr., Joe's love for the game always seemed to extend beyond his work between the lines.

In the final game, DiMaggio made a sensational catch in center field for the last out. Afterward, President Franklin D. Roosevelt, who attended the game, threw him a salute from the motorcade as it departed the Polo Grounds. It was Joe's first run-in with a President, and it would not be his last.

The Yankees' sweep of the Giants was a hard pill to swallow for Giants manager Bill Terry. In summing up DiMaggio's contribution, Terry said, "I've always heard that one player could make a difference between a losing team and a winner, and I never believed it. Now, I know it's true."

Like a graceful and swift-sailing vessel, the Yankee Clipper confidently patrolled the vast outfield of Yankee Stadium for 13 seasons.

In his 13 major league seasons, many observers agree, DiMaggio represented the epitome of dedication and natural talent with an all-round quest for perfection in his day-to-day efforts. These attributes won him induction into the Hall of Fame in 1955. Even years later, DiMaggio proudly stood by remarks he made as a young player: "I'm just a ballplayer with only one ambition — to give all I've got to help my club win. I've never played any other way."

Like today's players, however, DiMaggio was not averse to seeking higher pay for his talents and, in a sense, resembled the superstars of this generation.

"You can never tell when something is going to happen," he said as a player, "something that will end your career. I don't believe in a player being selfish or placing too high a price on his services, but a fellow's a sucker not to try to get all he can. He may be a star one day and a cripple the next."

Joe was a holdout in 1938, seeking $40,000 in salary from Yankees owner Jacob Ruppert after hitting 46 homers in 1937, just his second season in the majors. Ruppert maligned DiMaggio in the press as an "ingrate" who should be happy making a living playing ball, especially when most young American men were looking desperately for work. Joe ended the holdout and settled for $25,000. Eventually, he would become the first major leaguer to sign a $100,000 contract.

DiMaggio often was injured or ill and missed valuable playing time. He had operations for bone spurs in his heels, he was out with leg, knee and ankle injuries, a burned foot, infected tonsils, an abscessed tooth, ulcers and pneumonia.

In 1949, after missing 65 games because of bone spurs, he rejoined the club in June in Boston and launched one of baseball's most scintillating comebacks. In a three-game sweep at Fenway Park, he rapped four home runs and drove in nine runs. Joe's immediate contributions catapulted the Yankees into the thick of the race and to another championship season. As a result of his success, Joe graced the cover of Life magazine.

Perhaps his greatest feat was hitting in 56 consecutive games in 1941, the same season Ted Williams batted .406, and the last summer before the United States entered World War II after the bombing of Pearl Harbor.

He began the streak on May 15, and in every game through July 16 he recorded at least one hit. Jukeboxes and radios everywhere blared, "Joe, Joe, DiMaggio, we want you on our side," lyrics from the song "Joltin' Joe DiMaggio," written during the streak and extolling his day-to-day exploits.

During the streak, DiMaggio posted 91 hits, including 15 homers, 16 doubles and four triples. He scored 56 runs and batted in 55. His batting average for that span was .408.

The streak ended during a night game in Cleveland on July 17. Indians

Joe's picture-perfect swing was a model of consistency envied by other hitters.

third baseman Ken Keltner robbed Joe of two would-be hits with sensational plays on hard-hit balls. The next day, he started another streak that lasted for 16 games. Thus, from May 15 to Aug. 3, DiMaggio hit safely in 72 of 73 games.

After that gripping campaign, he played one more season — a pennant-winning but World Series-losing one — before he answered Uncle Sam's call to join the Army Air Forces. He missed what should have been his peak seasons, from 1943 through 1945. What difference would those three seasons have made in his final statistics? Consider his career totals: a .325 batting average, 2,214 hits, 1,537 RBI, 361 homers, 389 doubles, 131 triples, 1,390 runs scored and 369 strikeouts — just 13 in 1941.

Had DiMaggio merely produced "average" statistics in the three seasons he missed, he easily would have topped the 400-homer mark and would have approached 2,000 RBI.

Although Williams easily outdistanced DiMaggio's .357 batting average in 1941, Joe won the second of three Most Valuable Player awards that season, chiefly on the strength of the streak and the Yankees' steamrolling ride to another pennant by 17 games. He captured the MVP Award in 1939 when he won the batting title with a .381 average, and he would be MVP again in 1947 — both pennant-winning seasons. In 1940, he won the batting title for a second straight season, with a .352 average, but no pennant came with it.

In all, DiMaggio played on 10 pennant-winning teams and nine World Series championship teams.

In 1977, he hobnobbed with another president when he received the Medal of Freedom, the nation's highest civilian award, given for distinguished contributions to the American way of life, from President Ford.

In 1988, President Reagan invited him to the White House to be among 126 guests at a formal dinner in honor of Soviet leader Mikhail S. Gorbachev.

"On the receiving line," DiMaggio says, "the greeter asks how you'd like to be introduced. I said, 'Just Joe DiMaggio.' Then the President introduced me to Mr. Gorbachev and said: 'This is one of our greatest players in the United States.' Mr. Gorbachev looked as though he knew me."

DiMaggio quickly took advantage of his popularity. He asked the two men to autograph a baseball.

"In my life," DiMaggio said later, "that's the only time I ever asked anybody to sign a baseball. But I was a witness to history."

And as a ballplayer and folk hero, Joe DiMaggio, too, has become part of American history.

George De Gregorio is a member of the sports staff of The New York Times and author of Joe DiMaggio, An Informal Biography.

Nearly 60 years after making his New York debut, Joe remains a revered figure at Yankee Stadium.

Once he discovered his calling on the city's sandlots,
Joe DiMaggio found himself recognized as a real . . .

San Francisco Treat

There was a time when Joe DiMaggio wasn't sure he wanted to be a baseball player.

He grew up playing baseball, basketball and tennis with neighborhood kids in the North Beach section of San Francisco.

"There was no grass," DiMaggio says. "We played [baseball] on asphalt, with a big ball — a softball — but we threw it overhand and played by regular baseball rules. When I was 11 or 12, I started playing with older fellas, guys in their 20s. I guess they saw something in me."

It was something he didn't yet see in himself.

He didn't play baseball from the ages of 14 through 16, because he wasn't particularly interested. Then Rossi Olive Oil, a Class B semi-pro team, was looking for a shortstop, and somebody said, "Hey, why not get Joe DiMaggio?"

In the playoffs that year, Joe hit two home runs against the Maytag washing machines team, and his team won the league championship.

"They gave us little hollow gold baseballs — for watch fobs or for belt

Joe's rocket right arm was only one of the reasons Yankees scouts were eager for DiMaggio to trade his San Francisco Seals pinstripes for theirs.

By Dwight Chapin

The sight of DiMaggio crossing home plate with ease became a familiar one for Seals fans.

trinkets," DiMaggio says. "It was the first award I ever got in baseball." Foreshadowing? Definitely.

The next season — 1932 — DiMaggio moved up to the "A" League with what he called "the real big boys" on the No. 1 diamond at San Francisco's Funston Field, and was given his first pair of new spikes for having the highest batting average for the season. "Six hundred and something," he says.

When his Sunset Produce team completed its season, the San Francisco Seals of the Pacific Coast League were still playing.

"Augie Galan got permission to go to Hawaii to play in a couple of exhibition games, and the Seals were left without a shortstop," DiMaggio recalls. "A scout named Spike Hennessy used to watch the sandlot play, and he asked my brother, Vince, who was already with the Seals, if I would mind coming out and playing the last three games of the season with them."

DiMaggio smiled.

"Like I was going to turn them down," he says.

By this time, Joe had no doubt about his ability as a hitter.

"I used to watch the PCL fellas play at Recreation Park," DiMaggio says. "I saw Howard Craghead, who was supposed to be one of the best pitchers in the league, and I knew I could hit his stuff. But I didn't run around telling people so."

His first at-bat was against veteran Ted Pillette.

"Frankly," he says, "I wasn't nervous. A little tense just being in the ballgame, but not nervous."

DiMaggio tripled to right center field.

His play in the field, however, hardly qualified as a success. If he had remained at shortstop, in fact, the majors might never have beckoned.

"I've yet to throw anybody out from shortstop," DiMaggio says. "My arm was very, very strong — strong enough to break the seats back of first base — but not at all accurate. I never did count the errors I made that first year."

Still, the Seals offered him a contract for the 1933 season, which paid him $225 a month.

Within just a few months, DiMaggio had undergone some physical changes that startled Seals owner Charley Graham.

"I'd grown several inches," DiMaggio says. "Graham said I looked like a young fawn chasing the ball, legs going every which way."

So Seals manager Ike Caveney quickly and wisely converted Joe into an outfielder.

"The outfield was a natural place for me," DiMaggio says. "I could throw strikes to home plate from wherever I was out there."

DiMaggio continued to blossom as a hitter, too. Just 63 games into his professional baseball career, he began what would become a league-record 61-game hitting streak.

"Nobody asks about that much anymore," he says. "About the only place you see any mention of it is in the sports oddities section of newspapers. It's the streak in 1941 that everybody remembers. But the one in the Coast League did prepare me for the other streak, because it concentrated attention on me and gave me the chance, at 18, to accustom myself to outside pressures and separate them from the playing of the game."

San Francisco mayor Angelo Rossi presents Joe with a commemorative gold watch after Game 50 of his 61-game hitting streak with the Seals in 1933.

Players still marvel at DiMaggio's PCL record.

"He earned everything he got during that streak," said Bill Raimondi, who was the Oakland Oaks catcher at the time. "On the one hand, we hated it when he got hits against us, but we knew how much it meant to the teams in the league, too, because he put fans in the seats, and there weren't too many people coming to ballparks during the Depression. So whenever he got a hit, deep inside we had to be saying, 'Thank you, Joe.'"

DiMaggio went 104-for-257 for an average of .405 during the streak. As a token of the city's appreciation, San Francisco mayor Angelo Rossi presented him with a gold watch.

Although all 16 major league teams showed interest in bidding for Joe following his fine 1933 season, Graham wasn't ready to sell him.

One June night in 1934, DiMaggio had dinner with a sister and was heading home in a jitney cab. Space was cramped. He sat in an awkward position and didn't realize his left foot had fallen asleep. When Joe jumped out of the cab, his knee buckled and he went down as if he'd been shot.

"I heard four sharp cracks," he says. "It was really painful. It felt like I had a whole set of aching teeth."

He tried to play the next few days — he even managed a pinch-hit home run and a double — but he couldn't run, and a doctor diagnosed the injury as torn ligaments and placed DiMaggio's leg in an ankle-to-buttocks cast for six weeks.

"When they took it off, I couldn't bend the knee," he says. "To this day, I can't do a full knee bend."

Fifteen major league teams decided DiMaggio was washed up at the age of 19 because of the bad leg. But New York Yankees scouts Joe Devine and Bill Essick thought otherwise.

The Yankees offered $25,000 and five players for him, with the stipulation that he play center field for the Seals in 1935, and report to the Yankees in 1936.

He had hit .340 in 1933, .342 — despite the injury — in 1934 and .398 in 1935.

He clearly was ready for the majors.

Dwight Chapin is a sportswriter for the San Francisco Examiner.

After three seasons of development with the Seals, DiMaggio packed his bags for New York and was ready to go places with his career.

UPI / BETTMANN

Instant Stardom

Joe DiMaggio achieved star status and celebrity as a Yankee in a New York minute, then capped his pre-war career with his signature achievement

A couple of hundred years hence, when humans are taking bargain-rate, interplanetary excursions to Mars and beyond, the entry "DiMaggio" will bring one notation glowing onto their super-galactic laptop computers — Hit in 56 straight games in 1941.

Since that feat remains his signal career achievement, even more so than Joe's three Most Valuable Player awards and his lordly total of nine World Series championships in 10 appearances, the hitting streak naturally was the high point of his pre-war Yankees years. *(For more on DiMaggio's 56-game hitting streak, please see page 31.)*

In fact, the hitting streak became his calling card for Cooperstown. DiMaggio's Hall of Fame plaque features his full-face adult representation and just eight lines of type. None are more significant than the first two, which read:

"Hit safely in 56 consecutive games for major league record 1941. . . ."

All this was scarcely predictable five years earlier when DiMaggio arrived, a highly touted young star out of the Pacific Coast League. Depending on your perspective, the Yankees either were welcoming Ruth's successor or blowing $25,000 in the form of a cash payment to the San Francisco Seals, plus five players off their top farm club.

In less than a year, Joe rose from the minor leagues to national celebrity in the '36 World Series.

By Harold Rosenthal

A key figure for the Yankees in acquiring DiMaggio was Bill Essick, their No. 1 man in the Far West. Essick, who operated out of San Francisco, at one time lived across the street from DiMaggio.

Known as a big-time gambler, Essick gambled on a doctor's judgment on DiMaggio's injured knee. Essick's risk? For one thing, probably his job with the Yankees, or maybe even his career as a scout. Major failures fared poorly in the bread-line days of the Depression.

As a kid not even old enough to vote, DiMaggio in 1933 hit .340 in his first full season with the Seals, went 61 games without failing to get a hit and became a sensation in that city by the Bay. The major league scouts came flocking. Discussion of the selling figure ranged up around $100,000. DiMaggio's older brother, Tom, was doing the advising, and he knew hot property when he saw it. The family also would be guaranteed

a piece of the selling price.

Then came the unthinkable in 1934. The kid hurt himself — not sliding or running or swinging — but by getting up funny from a cramped position in one of those jitney buses en route home after a game. Ligaments in his left knee "popped like a shot." For the next 70 games DiMaggio rested, knee in cast, his own bright future cast in more than a partial eclipse.

Other major league scouts quickly lost interest. Not Essick. He had the "best people" in the business have a look. Those were the days in orthopedics of quick slashing and big, half-moon scars. But in DiMaggio's case, doctors assured Essick that immobilization would allow the knee to heal. He went with that judgment, and further, convinced the hard-headed (and tight-fisted) Yankees boss, Ed Barrow, of its correctness. Even more importantly, Essick got the Yankees' new farm director, George Weiss, to agree to take a chance on DiMaggio. Barrow ultimately went along. He didn't have to hint what would happen to Essick if DiMaggio flopped.

So in the spring of 1936, DiMaggio accepted the Yankees' invitation to spring training in St. Petersburg, Fla. Based on his resounding success with the Seals, the media immediately tagged Joe as "the replacement for Babe Ruth." Such expectations would have crushed other rookies. But not Joe DiMaggio.

In his major league debut against the St. Louis Browns at Yankee Stadium, DiMaggio ripped two singles and a triple in six at-bats. He also moved gracefully and swiftly in the outfield, dispelling all rumors that his knee still had not healed fully. DiMaggio wasted no time in proving to the Yankees that he was worth Essick's gamble.

In addition to hitting .323 with 29 homers and 125 RBI, the Yankees' new star set American League rookie records for runs (132) and triples (15). Yankees fans immediately recognized DiMaggio as the missing link the team needed to return to the World Series for the first time in three seasons — a long drought by Yankees standards at that time.

Not only did the Yankees return to the World Series, they revived their dynasty by claiming each of the next four World Series. And if his rookie season wasn't impressive enough, DiMaggio dazzled baseball fans across America in 1937 with a .346 batting average, 215 hits, 167 RBI, and league-leading totals in runs (151) and homers (46).

The Yankees were virtually unbeatable during those half-dozen seasons leading up to the start of hostilities. The "It's like rooting for U.S.

DiMaggio, who was tabbed by the New York media as the next Babe Ruth, was greeted with high expectations by owner Jacob Ruppert (bottom left) upon arriving in Florida for spring training in 1936.

Steel" sentiment was to come up later. Their motto of the time was "Five O'Clock Lightning," meaning that the Yankees simply could never be considered beaten. They were at their most formidable late in the game with the afternoon shadows gathering in the cavernous ballpark in the Bronx alongside that rattling elevated line.

Joe tended to keep pitchers off balance, especially with an inviting path to hit back through the box.

One of the best methods to measure DiMaggio's true value to the Yankees during this particular stage of his career would be the annual

MVP balloting, that has been conducted by the national baseball writers since the 1930s.

In his rookie season DiMaggio managed to shoulder his way into eighth place, giving the Yankees three players in the top 10: Lou Gehrig finished at the head of the list, Bill Dickey in fifth and DiMaggio in eighth.

Only the Tigers' Charlie Gehringer accumulated more votes than DiMaggio the following year. Joe dipped to sixth in 1938, but his next three seasons were about as good as any. He won over Red Sox first baseman Jimmie Foxx in '39, finished third in '40, and then took the MVP trophy again in 1941 largely due to his hitting streak.

That season Boston's Ted Williams hit .406 — which hasn't been equalled by another hitter since — yet Ted finished a whopping 37 points behind DiMaggio in the 1941 MVP balloting.

Conceded Williams at the time, "I believe there isn't a record in the books that will be harder to break. [DiMaggio's hitting streak] may be the greatest batting achievement of all."

First, third and first in three successive MVP races. No wonder bands played "Joltin' Joe DiMaggio" (arranged by Les Brown and his band of Reknown) instead of "Off We Go, Into the Wild Blue Yonder" as baseball's No. 1 star marched off into the murky future.

Harold Rosenthal is a Florida-based freelance writer who was a lifelong newsman in New York covering the Yankees, Dodgers, Giants and Mets.

With the nation on the brink of a second world war, DiMaggio was sworn into the Army Air Forces only a year after his 1941 MVP and World Series championship season.

Magic Number

As the pressure mounted with each passing day,
Joe DiMaggio fashioned a feat for the ages —
his 56-game hitting streak

Joe's hitting streak reached 56 games on July 16, 1941, with a first-inning single vs. Cleveland. But just a day later, the record-breaking ride came to a sudden halt, making headlines nationwide.

Joe DiMaggio's 56-game hitting streak from May 15 to July 17, 1941, arguably represents the greatest single achievement in baseball history.

"Arguably" is the operative word.

Some would place Rogers Hornsby's cumulative batting average of .402 from 1921 through 1925 ahead of DiMaggio's streak. Others, designate Roger Maris' 61 home runs in 1961 as the greatest of all feats. Still others believe Hack Wilson's 190 RBI in 1930 or Orel Hershiser's 59 consecutive scoreless innings in 1988 tops them all.

But all of these records lay claim to breathing room — days of rest interspersed between days of energy. Not so with DiMaggio's hitting streak. Day after day, week after week, month after month, the streak continued, slowly building in intense, nail-biting pressure.

Pressure? The very word seems alien in reference to Joe DiMaggio.

By Michael Seidel

Joe did more than just cast a shadow on Willie Keeler's record 44-game hitting streak, he obliterated it.

Stone-faced and silent, he moved with deliberate grace and precision on a ball field. His wide stance was so balanced that his swing seemed effortless. His short stride kept his head level and allowed him to make bat contact almost at will.

A disturbed rhythm in a hitter's swing may give the first indication of pressure. But DiMaggio's rhythm at the plate never changed. His steely ability to put the ball in play was nothing less than phenomenal. He struck out just seven times during his entire hitting streak, and through the course of the entire season, struck out a paltry 13 times.

So how did the pressure of a streak affect a ballplayer like Joe DiMaggio?

"You bet, I felt the pressure," an animated DiMaggio says. "I thought I was getting an ulcer around game 40. I even changed the way I hit. I swung early in the count, and at pitches out of the strike zone. I wanted to swing, to get it done fast. What worried me most was getting walked, or getting so deep in the count that I tensed up."

DiMaggio's nerves of steel were put to the test by key moments, key games and key at-bats.

New York World-Telegram sportswriter Dan Daniel first picked up DiMaggio's streak at game 13 — May 28. Sports pages across the country began tracking it in earnest at game 18. DiMaggio remembers the beginning. "I knew I at least started hitting from the first game of the streak because I was coming out of a slump in which I couldn't buy a hit for a week. Bobby Feller of the Indians shut me down 0-for-4 the game before, and so I was happy enough to get a ground-ball single off Edgar Smith in the first inning of the next game [May 15], against the White Sox. That was a wild one — we lost, 13-1.

"But I only started counting the streak games after Dan Daniel picked it up. There was a Memorial Day double-header in Boston. The streak hadn't even reached 20, and I didn't want to play. I had a terrible cold and a sore neck. Couldn't even lift my arm to throw. But [Yankees manager] Joe McCarthy had some other players hurting and, really, I guess I did want to keep the streak alive. I told Phil Rizzuto at short to come out and help me with anything in center. I made three throwing errors that day, and played an easy single into a double. Four errors. Awful. That never happened to me before. And I just managed to keep the streak going with a windblown fly that Pete Fox couldn't chase down.

"At game 33, I got seven straight hits in Detroit," DiMaggio continues. "That's when I really began thinking seriously about the major league record. We were winning a lot of ball games, and I was hitting pretty well. The tension started building then, though."

DiMaggio's closest call came in game 38, a memorable one at Yankee Stadium against the lowly St. Louis Browns. The whole country was abuzz at the time because of the massive invasion launched in late June by the Germans against the Russians. DiMaggio's streak was becoming a diversion for ever-increasing war anxieties. Yankee Stadium had a policy of admitting servicemen free, and thousands showed up for a game in which Yankee pitcher Marius Russo took a no-hitter into the eighth.

The huge crowd could hardly care less about Russo's pitching because

Joe DiMaggio's
56-Game Hitting Streak Breakdown

GAME NO.	DATE	TEAM AND PITCHER(S)	AB	R	H
1	May 15	White Sox; Smith	4	0	1
2	May 16	White Sox; Lee	4	2	2
3	May 17	White Sox; Rigney	3	1	1
4	May 18	Browns; Harris, Niggeling	3	3	3
5	May 19	Browns; Galehouse	3	0	1
6	May 20	Browns; Auker	5	1	1
7	May 21	Tigers; Rowe, Benton	5	0	2
8	May 22	Tigers; McKain	4	0	1
9	May 23	Red Sox; Newsome	5	0	1
10	May 24	Red Sox; Johnson	4	2	1
11	May 25	Red Sox; Grove	4	0	1
12	May 27	Senators; Chase, Anderson, Carrasquel	5	3	4
13	May 28	Senators; Hudson	4	1	1
14	May 29	Senators; Sundra	3	1	1
15	May 30	Red Sox; Johnson	2	1	1
16	May 30	Red Sox; Harris	3	0	1
17	June 1	Indians; Milnar	4	1	1
18	June 1	Indians; Harder	4	0	1
19	June 2	Indians; Feller	4	2	2
20	June 3	Tigers; Trout	4	1	1
21	June 5	Tigers; Newhouser	5	1	1
22	June 7	Browns; Muncrief, Allen, Caster	5	2	3
23	June 8	Browns; Auker	4	3	2
24	June 8	Browns; Caster, Kramer	4	1	2
25	June 10	White Sox; Rigney	5	1	1
26	June 12	White Sox; Lee	4	1	2
27	June 14	Indians; Feller	2	0	1
28	June 15	Indians; Bagby	3	1	1
29	June 16	Indians; Milnar	5	0	1
30	June 17	White Sox; Rigney	4	1	1
31	June 18	White Sox; Lee	3	0	1
32	June 19	White Sox; Smith, Ross	3	2	3
33	June 20	Tigers; Newsom, McKain	5	3	4
34	June 21	Tigers; Trout	4	0	1
35	June 22	Tigers, Newhouser, Newsom	5	1	2
36	June 24	Browns; Muncrief	4	1	1
37	June 25	Browns; Galehouse	4	1	1
38	June 26	Browns; Auker	4	0	1
39	June 27	Athletics; Dean	3	1	2
40	June 28	Athletics; Babich, Harris	5	1	2
41	June 29	Senators; Leonard	4	1	1
42	June 29	Senators; Anderson	5	1	1
43	July 1	Red Sox; Harris, Ryba	4	0	2
44	July 1	Red Sox; Wilson	3	1	1
45	July 2	Red Sox; Newsome	5	1	1
46	July 5	Athletics; Marchildon	4	2	1
47	July 6	Athletics; Babich, Hadley	5	2	4
48	July 6	Athletics; Knott	4	0	2
49	July 10	Browns; Niggling	2	0	1
50	July 11	Browns; Harris, Kramer	5	1	4
51	July 12	Browns; Auker, Muncrief	5	1	2
52	July 13	White Sox; Lyons, Hallett	4	2	3
53	July 13	White Sox; Lee	4	0	1
54	July 14	White Sox; Rigney	3	0	1
55	July 15	White Sox; Smith	4	1	2
56	July 16	Indians; Milnar, Krakauskas	4	3	3
			223	56	91
Totals			223	56	91

DiMaggio was hitless to the point. The fans — especially the servicemen — came to the ballpark for the streak. All DiMaggio had managed in his three previous at-bats was a tapper bobbled for an error by Browns' shortstop Johnny Berardino.

With one out in the eighth and Red Rolfe on first, Joe nervously waited in the on-deck circle as Tommy Henrich stepped into the batter's box. Henrich had one thing on his mind: Don't bounce into an inning-ending double play. After consulting with McCarthy, Henrich laid down a sacrifice bunt, advancing Rolfe to second and eliminating the possibility of an inning-ending double play.

DiMaggio then walked to the plate for his last at-bat, stretching those powerful, sinewy arms to loosen up. The park hushed. Sports photographers lined the foul-territory area along the base paths. And Joe's Yankees teammates gathered at the top of the dugout steps, tapping their bats in unison on the concrete step.

DiMaggio was edgy at the plate, smoothing the dirt, setting up just right against the submarining Browns pitcher, Eldon Auker.

"I wanted this over fast," DiMaggio recalls.

Auker wound up and delivered a low, inside fastball. DiMaggio ripped and met it square, at the apogee of his swing. The ball shot on a line past Harlong Clift at third and rocketed into the left-field corner. When the dust settled, DiMaggio stood quietly, but happily, on second. The crowd and the thousands of servicemen erupted. Photographers' camera bulbs flashed for what seemed like minutes. Ballplayers danced in the dugout.

That single at-bat in game 38 was the first to turn the hitting streak into 1941's version of a pressure-packed media event.

The Yankees then took the show on the road to Philadelphia and Washington. Even today, DiMaggio still recalls how his stomach knotted tighter than a half hitch when he faced A's pitcher Johnny Babich one game before he would tie the modern-day record of 41 straight set by George Sisler in 1922.

"I was already wound up tight, and then I read in the papers that Babich said he was going to walk me every time," DiMaggio says. "The first time up, I popped up a pitch near my eyes. The next time, I took three balls — not one of them even close to the plate. When Babich came in with ball four — and it was ball four, about a foot outside — I stepped across the batter's box and hit a line drive two inches from his ear into center field. That was the most satisfying hit of the whole streak. And what a relief!"

DiMaggio was not the only one steamed about Babich's antics. The longtime manager of the Philadelphia A's, Connie Mack, was so upset he threatened to fine any of his pitchers who refused to challenge DiMaggio with legitimate stuff in or near the strike zone.

"DiMaggio is one of baseball's greatest players," Mack said, "and any of my pitchers who won't pitch to him won't pitch for me."

DiMaggio went on to explain what it was like in the double-header

DiMaggio tied Keeler's hitting streak record with a first-inning single to center field against the Red Sox at Yankee Stadium on July 1, 1941.

Streak Stats

Joe DiMaggio's batting statistics during his 56-game hitting streak:

◆ 223 at-bats
◆ 91 hits — 56 singles, 16 doubles, four triples and 15 home runs
◆ 56 runs scored
◆ 55 runs batted in
◆ .408 batting average
◆ 21 base on balls
◆ 7 strikeouts
◆ Yankees record during the streak: 41-13-2
◆ Yankees climbed from fourth place, 5-1/2 games back, at the beginning of the streak to first place, six games up, when the streak ended.

with the Senators that next day, when he would tie and then break Sisler's record.

"Tough," he says, simply. "The temperature was over 100 degrees. I tied the record in the sixth inning of the first game with a double off a Dutch Leonard fastball. He usually threw knucklers, but he tried to slip a fastball in.

"Then, son of a gun, someone stole my bat between games. Reached right over the railing and took it. I had the collar on me in the second game until my last at-bat. Tommy Henrich told me to try his bat — he had a hunch. So I took it. Red Anderson brushed me back with the first pitch. Then he put the next one over. I lined it to left for a clean single. That was it."

DiMaggio continues, "You'd think the pressure would ease up. But it didn't. The writers dug up Wee Willie Keeler's old-time record of 44 straight. When we played Boston at Yankee Stadium a couple of days later my brother, Dom, told me he hadn't even heard of the Keeler record until he got to the park that morning. I was lucky, though. I tied the record in a double-header, and broke it the next day in game 45 with a home run in the fifth inning to left. Ted Williams was in left that day. He had quite a year himself in 1941."

The games after Keeler's record were easier for DiMaggio. He had

Instead of sulking in the locker room following the termination of his streak, Joe celebrated his accomplishment with manager Joe McCarthy and teammates.

Pete Rose and Paul Molitor are the only players in the past 40 years to make a semi-serious run at DiMaggio's record. Rose hit safely in 44 consecutive games in 1978; Molitor put together a 39-game streak in 1987.

only his minor league record of 61 straight to shoot for, set in 1933 when he played with the San Francisco Seals. But the tense moments in the streak continued until he finally came up short during a famous night game in Cleveland.

With the nation's eyes turned toward Joe's hitting streak, attendance at Yankees games continued to rise. On July 17, a major league game night-record 67,468 fans packed into Cleveland's Municipal Stadium.

Although the 1941 Indians were not the best defensive team in baseball, they played like they were during game 57 of DiMaggio's streak.

In the first inning, Joe blasted a bullet down the third-base line. Off the bat, it seemed to be a sure base hit. But Indians third baseman Ken Keltner made a diving backhand stab and threw Joe out by a step.

Joe conceded that the building pressure of the streak and his nervousness caused him to swing at many pitches that were out of the strike zone.

On his second at-bat, Joe failed to put the ball in play. Indians pitcher Al Smith was booed heavily as he walked Joe on a 3-2 pitch in the fourth inning.

DiMaggio returned to the plate in the seventh. Still facing Smith,

American League's Longest Hitting Streaks

PLAYER, TEAM	YEAR	GAMES
Joe DiMaggio, NY	1941	56
George Sisler, STL	1922	41
Ty Cobb, DET	1911	40
Paul Molitor, MIL	1987	39
Ty Cobb, DET	1917	35
George Sisler, STL	1925	34
George McQuinn, STL	1938	34
Dom DiMaggio, BOS	1949	34
Hal Chase, NY	1907	33
Heinie Manush, WAS	1933	33
Nap Lajoie, CLE	1906	31
Sam Rice, WAS	1924	31
Ken Landreaux, MIN	1980	31
Tris Speaker, BOS	1912	30
Bing Miller, PHI	1929	30
Goose Goslin, DET	1934	30
Ron LeFlore, DET	1976	30
George Brett, KC	1980	30

UPI / BETTMANN

DiMaggio lined another screamer toward Keltner at third. Keltner, who had been playing deep down the line, fielded the ball cleanly and again threw Joe out by an eyelash.

With the Yankees leading, 4-1, in the eighth, DiMaggio approached the plate, still without a hit. Against reliever Jim Bagby, DiMaggio smashed a fastball toward the left side of the infield.

"I hit it as hard as I ever hit any ground ball," Joe says.

Shortstop Lou Boudreau broke quickly on it and, despite the ball taking a nasty hop, snatched it off his shoulder and turned it into a 6-4-3 double play. The streak had ended.

Joe signals "goose eggs" after Cleveland held him hitless for the first time in 56 games.

Although he expressed a sense of disappointment, DiMaggio was glad to have a yoke of pressure lifted off his shoulders.

Not one to rest on his laurels though, DiMaggio began another hitting streak the next day that didn't end for another 16 games. In all, Joe had hit safely in 72 of 73 games from May 15 through Aug. 2.

The focus on the individualized drama of Joe's hitting streak then shifted to the team's drive toward another World Series title. The hubbub over Joe's streak — one of the most untouchable and phenomenal records in baseball — soon gave way to yet another Yankees championship.

Michael Seidel is a professor of literature at Columbia University and the author of Streak, Joe DiMaggio And The Summer of '41.

National League's Longest Hitting Streaks

PLAYER, TEAM	YEAR	GAMES
Willie Keeler, BAL	1897	44
Pete Rose, CIN	1978	44
Bill Dahlen, CHI	1894	42
Tommy Holmes, BOS	1945	37
Billy Hamilton, PHI	1894	36
Fred Clarke, LOU	1895	35
Benito Santiago, SD	1987	34
George Davis, NY	1893	33
Rogers Hornsby, STL	1922	32
Ed Delahanty, PHI	1899	31
Willie Davis, LA	1969	31
Rico Carty, ATL	1970	31
Elmer Smith, CIN	1898	30
Stan Musial, STL	1950	30
Jerome Walton, CHI	1989	30

Return to Glory

Despite personal anguish and physical pain,
Joe DiMaggio resumed his role
as leader of the powerful Yankees
upon returning from war duty

It was Alexander the Great who first observed, "Nothing's ever quite the same when you get back . . . but getting back is Job One." So it was with Joe DiMaggio, plus a few hundred other major league ballplayers, plus a few million American soldiers, men and women after the opposition finally was vanquished in World War II.

DiMaggio's ulcers got him back a little ahead of schedule, but he still sacrificed three seasons of baseball to the cause. He could have played some in '45, but he didn't feel right about it — not while the newspapers still were running casualty figures on Page 1. "Not when there are other guys still out there getting killed," was his sideline comment at the time.

The first year of the war, 1942, was a wrencher for a lot of people; DiMaggio was no exception. After the memorable 1941 season — highlighted by his 56-game hitting streak — Joe took notice of national and world belt-tightening. So he signed for merely a $5,000 raise.

During the 1942 season, he played in all 154 games for the first — and only — time. Yet it was a period of personal upheaval: the beginning of the end of his marriage to Dorothy Arnold. He participated in another World Series that year, but for the first time since 1926, the Yankees fell

By Harold Rosenthal

Although Joe was not quite the same player after returning from the services, he still maintained his powerful batting prowess, hitting 142 of his 361 career home runs after the war.

short in the Fall Classic. Then, against the backdrop of his wife's decision to hire a divorce lawyer, it was off to war.

He enlisted in the Army in December. In mid-January he and his wife met the press in Reno, hardly a place suggesting happily-ever-after, and they assured the press everything was going to be fine. It wasn't, of course.

In October, after Joe was in the military, Mrs. D. filed for divorce, charging cruelty and that Joe had "never acted like a married man."

The marriage never worked out. Today's prizes from that brief union are great-grandchildren old enough to wear toddler-size pinstripes at Yankees old-timers celebrations.

DiMaggio was not your average Army Air Forces enlistee. He played a little ball around the California bases before shipping out as a sergeant for the Seventh Air Forces Headquarters in Honolulu. There he joined a

Despite the happiness Joe and Dorothy Arnold shared after the birth of their child, Joe Jr., their marriage did not last.

group of ballplayers that could have given any of the remaining major-league clubs an interesting afternoon.

There wasn't a lot to do between ball games. A constant flow of New York writers on assignment for *Stars and Stripes* came through, and DiMaggio spoke with them about his marriage all the time.

Amid the confusion, the anxiety and stress, the facade around DiMaggio's nervous system cracked; he developed ulcers and was sent stateside. Just a few weeks before the '45 baseball season ended, Joe received his official discharge from military service.

Just as they had led their teams to the World Series in 1941, DiMaggio and Brooklyn shortstop Pee Wee Reese found themselves pitted against each other again just three years later at the Central Pacific Area Service championship game between the Seventh Army Air Forces and the Aiea Heights Naval Hospital team.

Fitting for his new start in 1946, DiMaggio returned to a new Yankees setup. The mercurial Larry MacPhail, a schemer, had put together a syndicate with multimillionaires Dan Topping and Del Webb that bought the Yankees from the cash-hungry Ruppert heirs. MacPhail wasn't one to argue with DiMaggio's demands. He wanted a winner, and after a stumbling start in '46 — a season in which DiMaggio hit .290 with 25 homers — the Yankees finished third behind Boston and Detroit.

In spring training of 1947, DiMaggio developed a heel problem and the season started without him in the lineup. DiMaggio soon made it back into the lineup, and played the rest of the season on a "bad gam," as he described it.

Even troubled by one leg, Joe was superior to anyone else in the league on two good ones, at least according to the writers in the Most Valuable Player balloting. DiMaggio, who hit .315 with 20 home runs and 97 RBI, edged Boston's Ted Williams by one vote. It was the last of his three MVP awards, a feat no player has topped.

The Indians beat every team in the league in 1948, in everything from the World Series to attendance. It was to be the Yankees' only World

Despite feeling the aches and pains of minor injuries, Joe willingly sacrificed his body in order to make the big plays.

Series absence for the rest of DiMaggio's baseball career. A switch of managers in 1949 brought in Casey Stengel, who immediately led the Yankees to five consecutive World Series championships, including DiMaggio's final three.

The thrills of 1949, enough perhaps to fill the life of an average player, constituted just another remarkable chapter in Joe's career — despite an inauspicious beginning. The heel acted up again. He missed the opener, and medical treatment continued to be ineffective. Even with half of Johns Hopkins on the job, Joe was unable to put any weight on it without experiencing exquisite agony.

He holed up in his hotel in New York rejecting everyone, staring no further than the box scores in the newspapers strewn around his room. Then, in a scene fit for the movies, he got up one morning and prepared to struggle to the bathroom. Instead he walked — without pain. He shaved in record time; there were things to do, like going after the pace-setting Red Sox as if they were cornered prey.

Looking much like the ragged and bloody continentals of the American Revolution, the Yankees nevertheless caught the Red Sox and beat them on the last day for the pennant. Gus Mauch, the club trainer, counted 72 injuries sustained during the season going into that momentous final game. And at the moment of victory the number increased to 73. Bill Dickey, one of Stengel's coaches, leaped in joy and paid for it with a cracked skull after slamming into the concrete roof of the dugout. What a bizarre scene resulted: Dickey out flat while the pinstripers celebrated around him.

After that, winning the World Series from the Dodgers was a breeze — the Yankees prevailed in five games. Despite still feeling the effects of a late-season viral infection, DiMaggio forced his weary body into the

The images of Yankee Stadium and Joe DiMaggio will be forever linked following the Yankee Clipper's 13 seasons of spectacular play.

Following his sudden recovery from heel injury in 1949, Joe led the Yankees' late-season charge to another World Series championship.

lineup for each game. And although Joe struck out five times and contributed just two hits in 18 at-bats, his mere presence on the field inspired and motivated his Yankees teammates.

Playing as baseball's only $100,000 man in 1950, DiMaggio justified his paycheck by batting .301 with 32 homers, 122 RBI and a league-leading .583 slugging percentage.

The next season — 1951 — was another in which the smart money picked the Yankees to finish behind Boston. It also was the one in which DiMaggio's successor showed up in Phoenix in the spring carrying the rube's traditional straw suitcase. Mickey Mantle played in right field most of that season, with DiMaggio patrolling his traditional spot in center.

Before the season started, though, DiMaggio abruptly announced late one Saturday night at spring training that 1951 was to be his last season.

Guiding DiMaggio's decision to retire was the 1950 MVP balloting: Phil Rizzuto, first; Yogi Berra, third; Vic Raschi seventh — teammates all ahead of him. The Yankee Clipper no longer was indispensible.

At the conclusion of the season, the Yankees made a big event DiMaggio's retirement, which had been an open secret for six months. The big press conference was highlighted by the revelation that there was another $100,000 contract waiting for him on the general manager's desk. No conditions — all he had to do was sign, and show up.

The Yankee Clipper politely declined, thanked one and all, and made his farewells. He passed from the role of box-office lure to baseball legend in the time it took for the elevator to descend from the 46th floor in New York's Squibb Building to street level and Fifth Avenue.

Harold Rosenthal is a Florida-based freelance writer who was a lifelong newsman in New York covering the Yankees, Dodgers, Giants and Mets.

Even though the pain of being out of the lineup and off the field was as great as the pain in his heel, Joe kept his spirits high.

Legend of the Fall

During his 13-season career,
Joe DiMaggio led the Yankees to an amazing
nine World Series crowns in 10 appearances

By Maury Allen

Joe receives congratulatory handshakes from his teammates after blasting a two-run homer into the upper deck of the left field bleachers during Game 4 of the 1951 World Series at the Polo Grounds in New York (left).

1936

Joe DiMaggio joined the Yankees as one of baseball's most heralded rookies. He had starred for the San Francisco Seals and in 1936, a year out of the minors, DiMaggio found himself playing center field and batting third in baseball's most grand event.

In Game 1, the Yankees faced Carl Hubbell, the New York Giants' famed screwball-throwing lefthander. Hubbell limited the Yankees to seven hits in a 6-1 Giants triumph.

Not ones to sulk about their previous performance, the Yankees stormed back to tie the Series with a resounding 18-4 victory in Game 2. DiMaggio collected three hits in five at-bats in the rout.

The Yankees capitalized on the sudden shift of momentum by winning Games 3 and 4 before finally wrapping up the championship with a 13-5 victory in Game 6.

In the six-game Series, the Yankees' new star pounded out nine hits, including three doubles, and compiled a .346 batting average in the first of his 10 World Series appearances.

Slipping under the tag of Giants first baseman Bill Terry, Joe narrowly escapes being picked off in Game 6.

Yankees third base coach Art Fletcher congratulates Joe following DiMaggio's Game 5 home run at the Polo Grounds.

1937

The Yankees and Giants met again in the 1937 World Series, and the results differed little from the previous year. The Yankees beat their rivals in five games with DiMaggio posting his first World Series homer in the final game of the Series. DiMaggio's home run, which came off Giants lefthander Cliff Melton in the third inning, sailed over the left field wall, giving the Yankees a 2-0 lead. The Bronx Bombers went on to a 4-2 victory and a second consecutive World Series championship.

DiMaggio hit .273 in the five-game series and again patrolled his position in center field flawlessly. In fact, the Yankees, as a team, did not commit a single error in the entire series, a World Series first.

In Game 1, although DiMaggio got two hits in four at-bats, he was the only Yankee in the lineup who did not score a run. Lefty Gomez pitched a complete game that day, as the Yankees set the tone for the Series early with a 8-1 rout over the Giants.

The scene wasn't much different in Game 2. The Yankees again limited the Giants to only one run in another 8-1 blowout victory. DiMaggio scored one run with his two hits in four plate appearances.

Sensing the humiliation of a four-game sweep following a 5-1 loss in Game 3, the Giants rallied for a 7-3 win in Game 4 in front of 44,293 fans at the Polo Grounds. That set the stage for DiMaggio's heroic Game 5 home run shot that sealed another Yankees title.

1938

The Yankees picked up where they left off the previous season and earned a third consecutive trip to the World Series. This time, the Chicago Cubs became the Yankees' victim.

In Game 2 of the Series, DiMaggio hit a two-run homer off Cubs righty Dizzy Dean in the ninth inning of a 6-3 New York triumph at Wrigley Field.

Dean, his famed fastball gone because of a midseason toe injury and subsequent arm trouble, had kept the Yankees to just two runs into the eighth. He threw mostly slow curves and changes to the slugging Yankees.

But New York shortstop Frank Crosetti homered off Dean in the eighth to put the Yankees ahead, and DiMaggio settled it with his two-run blast to seal the victory for Yankees starter Lefty Gomez.

The Yankees returned home to complete the sweep of Chicago and became the first club to win three consecutive championships.

A significant theme evolved from the 1938 World Series. DiMaggio, now completing his third professional season, was clearly the new star of the New York Yankees.

Lou Gehrig, showing signs of weariness and illness, finished the 1938 Series with four singles in 14 at-bats. It would be the last of Gehrig's seven World Series appearances. The leadership of the Yankees had quietly passed from Gehrig to DiMaggio.

AP / WIDE WORLD PHOTOS

Yankees right fielder Tommy Henrich receives a handshake from Joe after Henrich's homer in Game 4.

1939

The 1939 Yankees rivaled the 1927 Yankees as New York's best team ever, winning 106 games and taking the pennant over the Boston Red Sox by 17 games. They swept the Cincinnati Reds in four games as DiMaggio batted .313 with another Series homer to frustrate Bill McKechnie's Reds.

Yankees manager Joe McCarthy once said DiMaggio, to go along with all his other incredible skills, was the best base runner he had ever seen in the game. "He never made one mistake on the bases," McCarthy said. "If he went for an extra base, he made it."

That became clear in the 10th inning of the final game of the Series. The game had been tied, 4-4, going into the 10th as the Reds battled bravely to avoid the sweep. With Charlie Keller on second and DiMaggio on first, Yankees catcher Bill Dickey singled to right field. Right fielder Ivan Goodman juggled the ball as he tried to field it. Keller raced home. The throw to the plate was strong, and the play was close. Keller crashed into Ernie Lombardi, the huge Cincinnati catcher, and the ball was knocked free.

Keller touched the plate with the lead run and DiMaggio, seeing that Lombardi was still prone on the ground, raced all the way home with the extra run. That three-run 10th inning propelled the Yankees to the victory and another World Series championship.

Joe slides past Reds catcher Ernie Lombardi during a three-run 10th-inning rally in Game 4.

Joe DiMaggio   **51**

1941

The October Classic again returned to New York in 1941, when the Brooklyn Dodgers won their first pennant in 21 years.

The 1941 Series included one of the most bizarre plays in World Series history. And DiMaggio, of course, stood right in the middle of it.

The Yankees won the first game, and the Dodgers came back to win the second game, 3-2. When the Series moved to Brooklyn, the Yankees won, 2-1, with DiMaggio's RBI hit making the difference in a two-run Yankees eighth inning that opened up a scoreless game.

The Dodgers rallied the next day to lead, 4-3, with two out and nobody on in the top of the ninth. Tommy Henrich, the Yankees' right fielder known as Old Reliable for his famed clutch hits, stood at the plate against curveballing righty Hugh Casey.

Henrich, seeing a curveball with two strikes, swung at the pitch and missed. Umpire Larry Goetz threw up his right arm to signal strike three and the players came out of their dugouts, thinking the game was over.

But then, just as suddenly, Dodgers catcher Mickey Owen was chasing the ball. Henrich, dejected about the strikeout, heard his teammates screaming, looked around and spotted the ball heading for the wall.

Henrich raced to first base as Owen chased the ball. Henrich beat Owen's throw to first base, and the game was still alive. Owen came back to the plate, and Casey went back to the mound. Both seemed in shock.

The next hitter was DiMaggio, who cracked the first pitch from Casey into left field for a single. Charlie Keller followed with a double for two runs, Dickey walked, and Joe Gordon followed with another double scoring two more runs. The Yankees won, 7-4, after a shell-shocked Brooklyn team went out meekly in the bottom of the ninth.

The Yankees won the next day to clinch their fifth World Series triumph in DiMaggio's sixth season.

Joe scores the winning run in the ninth inning of Game 4 at Ebbets Field.

1942

In 1942, the Yankees' World Series dynasty stumbled. The upstart Cardinals shocked New York with four straight victories after the Yankees won the Series opener, 7-4.

DiMaggio registered a good Series with a .333 batting average, but St. Louis, the youngest team in the league, took the championship in five games. Joe's fine play had carried over from another great regular season in which he hit .305 with 21 homers and 114 RBI.

The turning point for St. Louis may have come with a spectacular defensive performance in a pivotal Game 3 at Yankee Stadium. With the Cardinals nursing a 1-0 lead in the sixth inning, St. Louis center fielder Terry Moore robbed DiMaggio of a base hit and a game-tying RBI with a beautiful diving catch. Then in the seventh, outfielders Stan Musial and Enos Slaughter preserved the St. Louis lead by robbing Charlie Keller and Joe Gordon of home runs on back-to-back at-bats.

Musial, only a rookie, played a key role for St. Louis at the plate in Game 4 by going 2-for-3 in a 9-6 victory.

World War II was taking a severe toll on baseball by 1943. The Yankees won another championship but the heart of the team, DiMaggio, now wore Army khaki.

Billboards at Sportsman's Park in St. Louis signified the sign of the times during the '42 World Series.

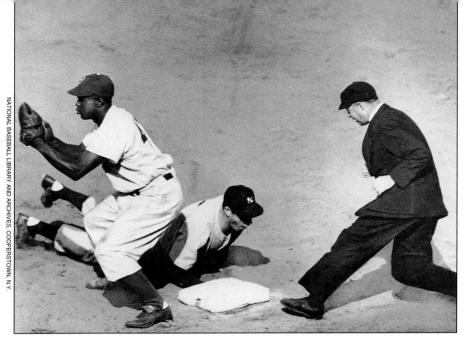

Joe dives back into first base as rookie Jackie Robinson, the first black man to play in a World Series game, takes the throw.

1947

In the season following his war duty, DiMaggio hit just .290, but rediscovered his old form in 1947 with a .315 batting mark, 20 homers and 97 RBI as the Yankees won the pennant again.

This season's matchup, between the Yankees and Dodgers, became the first-ever nationally televised World Series. And the broad television coverage captured the most expressive show of emotion by DiMaggio on a ball field in his brilliant Hall of Fame career.

The Yankees led three games to two as the Dodgers rallied for an 8-5 lead in Game 6. With two men on in the sixth inning, DiMaggio stepped in against Dodgers lefthander Joe Hatten and crushed a fastball to the deepest part of Yankee Stadium's left center field, about 415 feet away.

With the crack of the bat reserve outfielder Al Gionfriddo broke into a full sprint. His hat fell off and his glove went up just as he smashed into the low fence in front of the bullpen.

"I wasn't sure I could catch the ball," Gionfriddo recalled. "I just figured I'd keep running until I hit the fence."

Amazingly, the ball stuck in Gionfriddo's mitt for the out. DiMaggio, running hard to second base, looked up just as the crowd gasped. He saw Gionfriddo bounce against the fence just after catching the ball.

Uncharacteristically, DiMaggio, who never showed any emotion on the field — and little off it — slowed up, kicked the dirt in front of him and glared unbelievably at Gionfriddo.

"That catch made me," Gionfriddo said years later. "I made a lot of catches like that in my career but to make it in the World Series, on television, against the great DiMaggio, well that was something."

After the Dodgers beat the Yankees, 8-6, with Gionfriddo's catch shutting down the Yankees' momentum, New York came back in the seventh and deciding game and posted a 5-2 victory for DiMaggio's sixth title in seven World Series appearances.

1949

The Cleveland Indians won the American League pennant in 1948, so DiMaggio didn't return to the Fall Classic again until 1949. The opponent, as it now seemed so often, was Brooklyn.

DiMaggio was 34 years old during that Series and was coming off an injury-filled season. He had made his incredible comeback in Boston after missing about a third of the season with a heel injury, but still was suffering some pain as the Series began.

The '49 Series was the first for the Yankees under new manager Casey Stengel. Stengel replaced Bucky Harris, who was fired after New York finished third in 1948.

The Yankees won the first game of the Series 1-0 on a dramatic home run by Tommy Henrich in the bottom of the ninth. The Dodgers came back to steal Game 2 in Yankee Stadium by the same score one day later. But from that point on, it was all Yankees.

DiMaggio homered in the fourth inning of a 10-6 triumph over the Dodgers in the fifth and final game of the Series. He batted just .111 in those five games, but his presence on the field stimulated the Yankees, as it had all season long following his dramatic return.

Joe takes a cut during a ninth-inning at-bat in Game 4.

1950

The 1950 Series pitted the Yankees against the young Philadelphia team known as the Whiz Kids who had won the pennant on the final day of the season.

Perhaps DiMaggio's greatest World Series moment occurred in the second game. Allie Reynolds faced Robin Roberts in that game. Two of the toughest pitchers in baseball, Reynolds and Roberts, battled through nine innings to a 1-1 tie.

DiMaggio, hitless in four tries against Roberts, faced him again in the 10th inning. Darkness was quickly becoming a factor in old Shibe Park.

"I thought I could slip a fastball by DiMaggio," Roberts recalled. "He was slowing down a little by then. What I forgot was that by the 10th inning of a tough game I was a little slower myself."

DiMaggio connected with the fastball from Roberts on the fat of his bat and drove it into the upper deck for a game-winning home run.

He accumulated three other hits in the Series for a .308 average as the Yankees cooled off the young Phillies with a four-game sweep.

The Yankees were the champions for the second time in a row under Stengel. It was DiMaggio's eighth Series victory in nine tries.

Joe flies out to right field for the third out of the first inning of Game 3 at Yankee Stadium.

Joe lines a single to left field, breaking an 0-for-13 slump in the Series.

1951

The '51 Series began with the Giants, still high from their dramatic "Shot Heard 'Round the World" victory over the Dodgers, beating the Yankees, 5-1. The Yankees rebounded with a 3-1 decision in Game 2 but then fell to the Giants again in Game 3.

DiMaggio homered off Sal Maglie in Game 4 — won by the Yankees, 6-2 — and produced three hits in a Game 5 Yankees victory.

DiMaggio had indicated all season that he would retire. But the Yankees, certain they could sell a few more tickets, never accepted his decision.

The Yankees won the sixth and final game, 4-3. In the eighth inning, DiMaggio lined a double off the right center field wall. When he was thrown out at third on a fielder's choice, DiMaggio got up, dusted his uniform shirt off and jogged into the Yankees' dugout.

The fans, sensing that this would be DiMaggio's final World Series game, or any big-league game for that matter, stood as one to cheer him. It was a huge ovation for the famed Yankee Clipper, who touched his cap as he dipped his head into the Yankees' dugout.

His baseball life was done. He had played in 10 World Series, been on the winning side in nine of them, batted .271, hit eight home runs, played beautiful defense and graced the game with his presence.

Joseph Paul DiMaggio Jr. now was assigned to baseball lore.

Maury Allen covered the Yankees for the New York Post.

Best in the Business

Joe DiMaggio may have been best known for his hitting exploits, but it was his leadership skills, exceptional glovework and aggressiveness on the bases that earned him three MVP awards

To give you an idea of what kind of natural Joe DiMaggio was, he joined the Yankees in 1936 and there was no breaking-in period. You know how people say rookies have to get their feet wet? He was ready right from the beginning. And despite missing the first two weeks of the season [with an injured left foot], he gets three hits in his opening game with the Yankees, goes on to get 200 hits that season and then 200 hits the next season, as well.

Now, by the time he reaches the 1939 season, he's pretty much at his peak and he wins his first MVP. Despite the fact that he played just 120 games, he was voted the best player in the league. And despite the fact

**By Jerry Girard
as told to Mike Pagel**

that he played in just those games, he knocked in 126 runs and hit .381. That's amazing in itself when you figure this is a home-run hitter hitting for an average that high.

But it's even more amazing when you consider the dimensions of Yankee Stadium at that time — 457 feet to left center, 461 to dead center, 407 to right center. So you can imagine how many balls were caught at Yankee Stadium that would have been home runs anywhere else.

And so, he wins the MVP in '39. But also, the Yankees win the World Series for the fourth straight time. Back-to-back sweeps in '38 and '39. And DiMaggio becomes the first and remains the only player who began his career by winning the World Series his first four years.

The Yankees don't win [the World Series] in '40, but they come back in 1941 to win it again. And that was the year Joe won his second MVP. And this one had some controversy connected with it.

That was the year [Red Sox outfielder] Ted Williams hit .406. And some people thought that if you hit .400, you're automatically the MVP.

But not that year. Because that was also the year DiMaggio hit in 56 consecutive games, hit above .400 during that period, had more RBI than Williams — 125 to lead the league — and struck out just 13 times for the whole season.

So it was close, and you can see an argument for either side. But really, since the Yankees also won the pennant again that year, I think DiMaggio had the edge.

And then, Joe goes to war. He comes back, has an off-year in '46, and then in '47 wins MVP for the third time. And this one had even deeper controversy.

It was a subpar year for DiMaggio. He just barely hit 20 home runs and hit under 100 RBI. That same year, Ted Williams won the Triple Crown. [Williams] won the Triple Crown but didn't win the MVP. He really deserved it.

MVP Balloting Results

1939 American League		1941 American League		1947 American League	
J. DiMaggio, NY	280	J. DiMaggio, NY	291	J. DiMaggio, NY	202
J. Foxx, BOS	170	T. Williams, BOS	254	T. Williams, BOS	201
B. Feller, CLE	155	B. Feller, CLE	174	L. Boudreau, CLE	168
T. Williams, BOS	126	T. Lee, CHI	144	J. Page, NY	167
R. Ruffing, NY	116	C. Keller, NY	126	G. Kell, DET	132
B. Dickey, NY	110	C. Travis, WAS	101	G. McQuinn, NY	77
E. Leonard, WAS	71	J. Gordon, NY	60	J. Gordon, CLE	59
B. Johnson, PHI	52	J. Heath, CLE	37	B. Feller, CLE	58
J. Gordon, NY	43	H. Newsome, BOS	32	P. Marchildon, PHI	47
M. Kreevich, CHI	38	R. Cullenbine, SL	29	L. Appling, CHI	43

The maximum possible point total that could have been earned (by receiving the first-place nomination of every writer polled) is 336.

The first step of Joe's MVP seasons began at spring training where the Yankee Clipper honed his vicious and lethal swing.

So why didn't he get it? The answer was simple: He didn't get along with the writers. He didn't like them, they didn't like him, and since they voted, well, he was up the creek. So Williams wins the Triple Crown, and DiMaggio takes the MVP.

But there was another reason. [The writers] were kind of enamored with DiMaggio's play. While Williams was just an ordinary fielder at best, DiMaggio was sensational. Williams was not a good baserunner. DiMaggio was great — not in stolen bases, but in running the bases well.

I used to see him go from first to third, and from second to home on balls that other players wouldn't have even tried.

I remember one day, he was heading for third base, and he saw that

DiMaggio's aggressive style of attacking the base paths drew praise from many MVP voters.

Casualties of War

Joe DiMaggio's three-year hiatus from baseball opened the door for other players battling for the game's top individual player award

By Mike Pagel

Although Joe DiMaggio missed three seasons during the prime years of his baseball career, he still won three Most Valuable Player awards in his 13 seasons with the Yankees.

One can only speculate as to whether DiMaggio would have won another MVP Award had he not gone into the Army Air Forces. It's hard to argue against the kind of seasons MVP award-winning pitchers Spud Chandler and Hal Newhouser had during the seasons DiMaggio was away.

Chandler, DiMaggio's longtime teammate, posted a 20-4 record with a 1.64 ERA in 1943. The 36-year-old righthander also played a key role in leading New York to another World Series title. Chandler edged Chicago shortstop Luke Appling for the award that season.

In 1944, Detroit's Newhouser went 29-9 with a league-high 187 strikeouts to capture the award over teammate Dizzy Trout, who won 27 games with a league-best 2.12 ERA. Just four points separated the two in the balloting.

Newhouser ran away with the MVP voting in 1945. The Tigers' southpaw posted a 25-9 record with league bests in strikeouts (212) and ERA (1.81). Newhouser also led the Tigers to 88 regular season wins and a World Series championship.

One can only wonder how Newhouser's statistics would have differed if he'd faced DiMaggio a few dozen times in each of those seasons.

Like Newhouser, many other players boast two MVP awards in their careers. But just a few players in the history of the game have taken a step further. Eight major league ballplayers have scored a hat trick with the MVP Award in their careers. Including DiMaggio, four played in the American League, while four earned their awards in National League play.

San Francisco's Barry Bonds now appears to have the best chance to become the first four-time MVP winner.

The rundown of baseball's three-time MVP Award winners:

American League

Jimmie Fox, Philadelphia 1932,1933; Boston 1938
Joe DiMaggio, New York 1939,1941,1947
Yogi Berra, New York 1951, 1954, 1955
Mickey Mantle, New York 1956,1957,1962

National League

Stan Musial, St. Louis 1943,1946,1948
Roy Campanella, Brooklyn 1951,1953,1955
Mike Schmidt, Philadelphia 1980,1981,1986
Barry Bonds, Pittsburgh 1990,1992; San Francisco 1993

the throw was coming in on the left field side of third base, so he faded away to the home plate side of the third base and evaded the tag. And he could do that beautifully from both sides. He was a great fadeaway slider.

And, of course, he was a terrific all-around outfielder.

I think it's a toss-up between Mays and DiMaggio as to who's the best player I've ever seen play center field.

Just to give you an idea of what Joe could do in center field, I recall one time sitting in the right center field bleachers. The Yankees had the game wrapped up. A guy in the ninth inning hit a ball and you knew, with the crack of the bat, that this was high and far to dead center. Well, I immediately looked down at DiMaggio. He already had his back to the plate, racing full speed toward the flagpole. He never once looked back over his shoulder, just kept sprinting. At the last possible second, he reached out as far as he could, and the ball went off his glove. He didn't make the catch, but on the way home, I couldn't get it out of my mind. [It was] the greatest catch that was never made.

And that's the kind of thing that mesmerized the writers. And if you saw Joe DiMaggio play for one full season, you would have been mesmerized, too.

Jerry Girard worked as a sportscaster at WPIX-TV in New York for 20 years before recently retiring.

Baseball fans enjoyed many splendid moments as DiMaggio and Ted Williams jockeyed for the game's top individual honor.

A Star Among Stars

Joe DiMaggio may not have been a standout in All-Star games, but his experience as a winner brought success to the American League effort

Had it not been for Joe DiMaggio, the most dramatic moment in All-Star Game history might never have occurred.

On July 8, 1941, at Detroit's Briggs Stadium, Ted Williams blasted a three-run homer with two out in the bottom of the ninth, turning a 5-4 National League lead into a 7-5 American League victory.

Williams made the hit. But DiMaggio made it possible.

DiMaggio, just moments before the game-winning homer, kept the game alive by beating out a throw to first base on a 6-4-3 double-play attempt.

That moment symbolizes an aspect of DiMaggio seldom appreciated by many who praise him so highly for his other, more obvious, baseball virtues. He wasn't the star of the occasion, he didn't get the key hit, he didn't produce singlehanded heroics; he just helped his team win the game.

By Leonard Koppett

Former New York Yankee Tommy Henrich likes to tell the story of a group of Yankees comparing great ballplayers, and one of them singles out DiMaggio and says: "All I know, is that whenever he's on our team we win."

In his distinguished career, DiMaggio experienced few big moments in All-Star games — fewer than Williams, or Willie Mays, or Stan Musial or other stars. But somehow, the team he played for usually won.

He was selected to participate in the All-Star Game in each of his 13 major league seasons, but twice he didn't play — in 1946 because of an injury, and in 1951, his final season. Of the 11 games in which he appeared, the American League won seven, a .636 pace, good enough to win most pennants. In all the other All-Star games throughout history, the American League's record without DiMaggio on its roster is 19-34-1, a winning percentage of just .359.

Coincidence? Maybe. But facts tend to suggest otherwise.

Actually, some of DiMaggio's All-Star experiences could be considered among his more embarrassing moments in baseball. It was that way from the outset.

As the heralded Yankees rookie in 1936, Joe started the season a few games late because of a foot injury, but by July he clearly had earned the

In just his second year in the league, Joe already stood out as one of the most dangerous hitters in the American League's All-Star Game lineup, which also included (left to right) Lou Gehrig, Joe Cronin, Bill Dickey, Charlie Gehringer, Jimmy Foxx and Hank Greenberg.

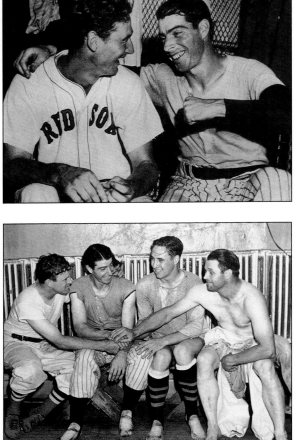

Joe maintained a friendly relationship with his All-Star teammates, including Ted Williams, who drove DiMaggio home with a game-winning home run in the ninth inning of the 1941 All-Star Game.

privilege of starting in right field. This was just the fourth All-Star Game, a glamorous novelty that the American League had swept in the first three seasons. The National League felt a desperate need to salvage prestige; for the American League, victory was taken for granted.

In the fifth inning, with the National League already leading, 3-0, Cubs second baseman Billy Herman singled to right and DiMaggio bobbled the ball, allowing Billy to take second. Herman, thanks to the only error in the game, then scored what turned out to be the winning run in the NL's 4-3 triumph.

At bat, Joe was hitless in five tries. In his last at-bat in the ninth, DiMaggio popped up with the tying run in scoring position.

Some debut. In those days, much was made of a "hero or goat" in every game. And in the 1936 All-Star Classic, DiMaggio was the goat.

But in 1937, at Washington's Griffith Stadium, Joe took advantage of his next opportunity to redeem himself among his peers.

St. Louis righthander Dizzy Dean walked DiMaggio in the first inning, but mowed down the remaining American Leaguers. In the third, Joe broke his All-Star Game drought by smashing a single through the box. Lou Gehrig followed with a titanic home run for a 2-0 lead in what became an 8-3 American League victory. In addition to his bat coming alive in that All-Star Game, DiMaggio's play in the field improved, too. The Yankees' center fielder threw a runner out at home to end the sixth inning.

In the 1938, '39 and '40 games, DiMaggio again played well but his team came up short in two of the three contests. It was in the 1939 All-Star contest that DiMaggio hit a home run and led his American League squad to a 3-1 victory in front of nearly 63,000 fans at Yankee Stadium.

Then came that exciting All-Star Game of 1941.

By July 6, when the All-Star break arrived, DiMaggio had stretched his record-breaking hitting streak to 48 games.

As a matter of pride, it was important to keep the hitting streak alive in the "unofficial" All-Star Game. The National League successfully retired Joe in his first two at-bats and walked him in his third. But with one out in the eighth, Joe smacked a double and scored on brother Dom's single. Williams then provided for the ninth-inning dramatics with his game-winning home run.

Because of war duties and injuries, DiMaggio made just five more All-Star appearances in the course of the next decade. In those five games, the American League went 4-1 as DiMaggio averaged a hit per game.

Overall, Joe DiMaggio's All-Star statistics were monumentally unimposing. But then, no championships are at stake in All-Star games.

In his 11 games as an All-Star, DiMaggio hit just .225. But in his grand total of 51 World Series games, he batted .271 and averaged more than a hit per game. Throw in DiMaggio's .325 career average in 1,736 regular season games, and his consistency as a hitter becomes quite obvious.

The more he played, the more he produced. But what else would you expect from the man who hit safely in 56 consecutive games?

It all boils down to definitions. The All-Star Game is not the place to show you're a star; it's where you play because you are a star.

In astronomy, the brightest stars are called "first magnitude." Anything brighter is measured as zero or minus-number magnitude. In comparison with the brightest stars, Joe DiMaggio ranks as at least a zero.

Leonard Koppett, an active baseball writer since 1948, spent 30 years writing for several New York newspapers and currently writes a column for the Oakland Tribune.

Proving to his peers that he had completely recovered from his heel injury, DiMaggio doubles during the 1949 All-Star Game at Ebbets Field in Brooklyn.

George Humes

Appreciations of Artistry

Befitting a baseball legend whose playing style often
was described in artistic terms, we present tributes
from a variety of artists who capture the
special essence of Joe DiMaggio

Jeff Suntala

Opie Otterstad

Darryl Vlasak

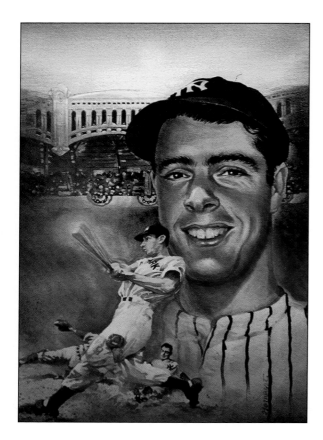

John Gampert

Murray Tinkelman

A Brotherhood of Talent

Vince, Joe and Dom DiMaggio
shared the same name and the same dream
— to reach the big leagues

Just where do you start with Joe DiMaggio?

Here's a man who's been called the greatest player ever. And why not? He hit in 56 consecutive games, won three Most Valuable Player awards, played on the winning side in nine World Series and, as a popular song of the era raved, "glorified the horsehide sphere."

There must be a million memories.

But all of that fame and glory, all the awards and honors, just may take a backseat to a single at-bat in 1941 — a plate appearance so satisfying the Yankee Clipper still recalls it with vivid detail, having watched the whole thing from second base.

Watched?

Indeed, it was brother Dominic DiMaggio who was swinging the bat. With Joe dancing off second base after doubling in the bottom of the eighth of the 1941 All-Star Game, Dom delivered a single to drive in his older brother.

"I believe it was the first time a brother drove in a brother in the All-Star Game," Joe says proudly.

Joe would return the favor eight years later, driving home Dom in the 1949 midsummer classic. The two brothers, Joe with the Yankees and Dom with the Red Sox, played alongside each other in the outfield in three different All-Star games.

There was another All-Star in the family. And although Vince

By Mike Payne

DiMaggio never got to share the outfield with his two ballplaying brothers, he did in fact appear in two All-Star games and was a pretty good fielder himself. Unfortunately for Vince, the oldest of the three ballplaying brothers, he also never met a pitch he didn't like. Unfortunately, many of those were out of the strike zone.

When all was said and done, Vince had led the National League in striking out in six of his 10 seasons in the league.

If Joe was the smooth Yankee Clipper, and Dom the talented and bespectacled Little Professor, then Vince DiMaggio was . . . well . . . perhaps the best cook of the family. He certainly was the most outgoing of the three ballplaying siblings.

But never mind the .249 average accumulated through his 10 seasons with five National League clubs, Vince was a DiMaggio. And without Vince, the world might never have heard of Joe.

Oh, Vincent had his moments of glory. He slugged 21 homers and col-

As the most successful of the DiMaggio brother trio, it only was natural that Joe took his brothers, Vince (left) and Dom, under his wings.

lected 100 RBI for the Pittsburgh Pirates in 1941. He also was considered by opponents as one of the NL's best base runners.

But timing never seemed to work in Vince's favor. His two All-Star appearances came in seasons when Joe and Dom were both off to war. Yet Vince still managed to make a name for himself by going 3-for-3 with a home run and a triple in the '43 game, proving that baseball — even if just for a short period — could offer headlines to yet another DiMaggio.

Vince also is the first of the three to actually get paid as a professional, earning a wage with the San Francisco Seals of the Pacific Coast League in 1932. And a funny thing happened on the way to the end of that '32 season — the Seals found themselves without a shortstop when their regular left the team to travel to Hawaii three days before the season finale.

When Vince learned of the situation, he offered the services of his younger brother, Joe, to the team. Although no one had ever heard of "Vince's brother," the Seals needed someone to play shortstop. The club took Vince up on his offer, and the next day 17-year-old Joe showed up with cleats, a glove and a bat. With Vince in right field, Joe handled the shortstop duties for the final three games, making only one error. But more importantly, he raised eyebrows at the plate by collecting a double and a triple with two RBI in nine at-bats.

From that point on, Joe D was in baseball to stay, being paid the princely sum of $225 per month to play for the Seals the next season — great money at the time. Three years later, he would star in Yankee Stadium.

The DiMaggio brothers rarely passed up a chance to pursue their passion for baseball, even fashioning makeshift games behind the family restaurant in San Francisco.

Dominic DiMaggio could not be any more different than Joe. With his smallish frame and ever-present glasses, Dom looked more the part of a bookworm, and he lacked the power of Joe and Vince. But he was fast — very fast — and many who saw both Dom and Joe patrol center field for their respective clubs characterized Dominic as the more graceful player.

He spent a productive 10-season career with the Red Sox, and actually played three games of an 11th season before calling it quits in 1953. Not only did he share the Boston outfield with Ted Williams, but the Splendid Splinter called Dominic one of the finest fielders he'd ever seen.

The three DiMaggios never did play in the same major league outfield, but did get together once in 1956, when they played for the

Seals Old-Timers in an exhibition game. Vince played left, Dom was in center, and Joe was in right. After that, the three went on to live separate lives.

"I'm not sure they were ever that close," says former New York Post sportswriter Maury Allen, a longtime DiMaggio acquaintance and author of the book, *Where Have You Gone, Joe DiMaggio?* "They traveled different paths."

Allen, who interviewed Joe and Dom for his book, also requested an interview with Vince, but the third brother turned him down because of health reasons. Vince passed away in 1986. "Joe has grown closer to Dominic now," Allen says. "They were just different people. Joe dated models and actresses. Dom is kind of refined and has been married to the same woman for 45 years.

"As for three brothers making the major leagues, no other siblings can compare," Allen continues. "You've got Joe, one of the greatest ever; Dom, who was a good ballplayer and who Ted Williams said was every bit the fielder Joe was; and Vince, who was a decent ballplayer himself.

"That ain't bad, is it?"

Three boys from the same family accounting for 22 All-Star Game appearances and a place in baseball history?

Not bad at all.

Mike Payne is a managing editor at Beckett Publications.

Gene and Bill Lillard (left) joined Dom and Joe as brothers who made it to the big leagues through the San Francisco Seals' organization.

An Everlasting Love

Although Joe's marriage with Marilyn Monroe
didn't last, his love for her lives on

Joe and Marilyn. Marilyn and Joe. One hardly knows which name to put first.

On the surface, central casting could not have asked for more. They were young, handsome and known by millions. In 1954, Joe DiMaggio, two years into his baseball retirement, and Marilyn Monroe, already well on her way to becoming the era's preeminent screen goddess, were the grist of the gossip mill. He had been the nation's greatest ballplayer, she was fast-becoming America's leading sex symbol. Columnists from New York to Los Angeles dubbed their love the "Romance of the Century."

It was a heavy burden to carry. And, it is one to this day that the Yankee Clipper endures in relative silence.

Although congenial to the press, he always has been wary of reporters he does not know well. And even to those he has befriended through the

By Barry Schatz

Two of America's most-loved celebrities exited San Francisco's City Hall as America's most intriguing couple following their wedding in 1954.

years, he never speaks publicly about his nine-month marriage to Monroe or their ensuing relationship, which lasted for a decade until her death from an overdose in 1962.

To the end, through all Marilyn's rumored affairs, insecurities, hospitalizations for depression and other mental disorders, DiMaggio remained a trusted and valued friend to her, and she the love of his life.

I t all began in the winter of 1951-52, when DiMaggio, reportedly after seeing a photograph of the blonde starlet, asked to meet her.

Reports conflict on whether she knew who he was. She knew little of his sport, the kingdom he ruled for so many years.

"I was surprised to be so crazy about Joe," she related to her longtime confidant Milton Greene, according to Donald Spoto's book, *Marilyn Monroe — The Biography*. "I expected a flashy New York sports type and instead I met this reserved guy who didn't make a pass at me right away. I had dinner with him almost every night for two weeks. He treated me like something special. Joe is a very decent man, and he makes other people feel decent, too."

Their marriage took place at San Francisco City Hall on Jan. 14, 1954. It was the second marriage for both, and because the Catholic Church did not recognize divorce, Joe's request for a priest to do the honors was turned down by the archbishop of San Francisco. News of their marriage splashed onto front pages across the country with the photo of a radiant, curvaceous movie star kissing a baseball hero accompanying it. A marriage made in heaven, or so it seemed.

But there were problems. They were different ages — he was a dozen years her senior — and came from very different backgrounds. By all accounts, he had a traditional view of women, one that was not unlike that of many first-generation Italian-Americans at the time who had worked their way up from humble beginnings. It was one in which women acted modestly, kept a neat house, supported their husband's efforts and stayed at home to comfort and nurture their family. Immodest behavior would not do.

This expectation was nothing like what DiMaggio's new bride had experienced in her youth, nor what she apparently desired as an adult.

Born to a struggling woman who was institutionalized much of her adult life, the former Norma Jean Baker survived a Dickensian childhood. There was not a father around and, within 11 days after her birth on June 1, 1926 in Los Angeles, Monroe was shipped off to a foster home,

AP / WIDE WORLD PHOTOS

Although Joe preferred a more private lifestyle, he and Marilyn occasionally enjoyed a night on the town during their nine-month marriage.

the first of many at which she would reside.

Insecure and filled with self-doubt, she brought into adulthood a need to be desired, respected and adored. There had been a calendar with risqué photos of her, more than a dozen movies and the publicity machine of Hollywood pushing her celebrity more and more by the time Monroe and DiMaggio wed.

Joe loved Marilyn, but he seemingly hated all the rest. He was skeptical of Hollywood and didn't want any part of it. He liked sitting home, watching television at night, or meeting with the guys. She wanted to socialize with show business types, have friends over, be shown attention. They lived in two worlds, incompatible from the start.

It didn't take long for things to fall apart.

The final straw came while she was shooting the now-famous skirt-blowing scene for *The Seven Year Itch* on a busy New York street. DiMaggio, apparently unaware of the provocative nature of the action about to take place in which Monroe's skirt would be blown above knee level, was taken aback.

"What the hell's going on around here?" an angry DiMaggio asked before storming off. Two weeks later, Monroe filed for divorce. DiMaggio did not contest it.

Whitey Snyder, Monroe's longtime makeup man, is quoted as saying "She was very upset about the DiMaggio dilemma" in *Marilyn The Last Take* by Peter Harry Brown and Patte B. Barham. "Joe wanted to take her away from the degrading, demeaning Hollywood lifestyle. He wanted to give her a family life, values, security, her own house. But Marilyn was afraid to leave her career even though it brought her such turmoil."

After the divorce, they kept in touch off and on for the next eight years. She married noted playwright Arthur Miller, then divorced him. In the last 20 years, alleged affairs with both Robert and John F. Kennedy, Frank Sinatra and others have come to light. For his part, DiMaggio remained unattached.

And toward the end of her life, it was DiMaggio who was there for her at the key moments. When she wanted to end a very unhappy stay at the Payne Whitney Clinic, the psychiatric division of New York Hospital, in 1961, DiMaggio orchestrated her release and brought her to another facility. There he would stay with her until she regained her strength a few weeks later. When she later needed surgery to relieve a digestive tract illness, it was he who gave her support.

There was even talk before her death on Aug. 4, 1962, about them reuniting. Age apparently had mellowed both of them and instructed them in the value of each other. After her death, an unfinished letter from her to DiMaggio revealed her true feelings for him, according to Spoto's

Joe's enduring love for Marilyn became evident when he stepped forward and oversaw her funeral arrangements in 1962.

book. The following is an excerpt of Marilyn's letter to Joe:

"Dear Joe,

If I can only succeed in making you happy, I will have succeeded in the biggest and most difficult thing there is — that is, to make one person completely happy. Your happiness means my happiness, and . . ."

When it came time for someone to organize her funeral, DiMaggio stepped to the forefront. There would be no Hollywood types invited — no Sinatras, Lawfords or Kennedys. It would be a dignified ceremony, closed to the public, the way DiMaggio always liked things. Just a few dozen people would be allowed to attend.

"We hope that each person will understand that the last rites must of great necessity be as private as possible so that she can go to her final resting place in the quiet she has always sought," said a statement by DiMaggio, Monroe's half-sister, Bernice Miracle, and good friend, Inez Melson.

With hundreds of spectators waiting nearby, it was a teary-eyed Joe DiMaggio who stooped over her casket on Aug. 8, 1962 and kissed his Marilyn goodbye. "I love you," he said softly in a rare display of public emotion. "I love you."

For the next 20 years, a half-dozen long-stemmed roses from him would arrive regularly at her crypt three times a week. It was truly an eternal love that had touched them both.

Barry Schatz is a freelance writer in Springfield, Mass.

Link to Greatness

His unique status as the successor to Lou Gehrig
and the predecessor of Mickey Mantle
made Joe DiMaggio more than just another
link in the chain of Yankee greats

UPI / BETTMANN

Much the same way the young Joe DiMaggio took over the leadership reins from Lou Gehrig in the late 1930s, Mickey Mantle accepted the role of leader of the Yankees when DiMaggio retired after the 1951 season.

By Marty Noble

The assignment, as presented by a columnist in an airline travel magazine, was to submit lists of favorite things. Raindrops on roses and whiskers on kittens; stuff like that. A fun exercise even when you're on the ground. The writer promised to choose his favorites from among those submitted and publish them in a subsequent edition.

When he made good on his promise, he listed, among others, a first kiss, waltzing with grandpa, new underwear, the overwhelming smell of garlic cooking on olive oil and, also, my personal favorite from the list. From Virginia O'Neill-Houchin of Texas, two words: "Joe DiMaggio."

The columnist's favorites included other sports references — "Great NFL defense" and "Sitting in the bleachers in Wrigley Field on a sun-drenched afternoon." But no other sports celebrity was mentioned; no celebrity of any nature, for that matter. Just Joe D, Joltin' Joe, baseball icon, American institution, national resource, universal hero.

No explanation necessary. If you ever had watched Yankees baseball in the '30s and '40s — that is, after The Babe and The Iron Horse and before The Mick, no explanation is required. Nor would it be necessary for Ms. O'Neill-Houchin to explain her entry if you ever have spoken with a '50s father who had experienced the aura of The Yankee Clipper, the third in the sequence of extraordinary stars in the Yankees' unequaled galaxy.

Wearing No. 5 on his jersey, Joe followed Ruth's No. 3 and Gehrig's No. 4 and preceded Mantle's No. 7.

Of course, he didn't merely serve as a link between Gehrig and Mantle or as a custodian of the tradition begun by Ruth and extended by Gehrig. DiMaggio's presence coincided with the restoration of the Yankees. But it was not coincidental. Because of him more than any other player, the Yankees returned to dominance and prominence with the second of three stages of dominance that eventually made the franchise the most storied and accomplished in professional sports history.

Indeed, the Yankees won more World Series titles (nine) and league pennants (10) in Joe's 13 seasons than they had during Ruth's 15-season tenure with the team — four and seven, respectively. In Gehrig's 14 seasons as a full-time player, the Yankees won six World Series and seven league championships. During Mantle's 18 seasons in New York, the Yankees won pennants in 12 of the first 14 seasons and the World Series in seven of the 12.

DiMaggio's rookie season, 1936, marked the Yankees return to first place after a three-year absence, but it also marked just their second league championship in eight years. With that record, even after winning six pennants from

In sartorial matters, Mickey could not go wrong by consulting Joe, who once was named to the top 10 list of best-dressed men in America.

1921 through 1928, they had become mortal, even with the immortal Gehrig in the lineup.

Enter Joe D, and the Yankees win the six pennants and five World Series in seven seasons, a remarkable sequence that re-established the franchise and re-introduced the concept of a dynasty to baseball.

Gehrig was voted the Most Valuable Player in 1936, a season in which five Yankees drove in more than 100 runs. But DiMaggio's contributions as a rookie — .323 average, 44 doubles, 29 home runs, 132 runs and 125 RBI — couldn't be overlooked.

Though the torch, lit by Ruth in the '20s, eventually would be passed from Gehrig to DiMaggio (and then to Mantle), it wasn't Gehrig who ushered DiMaggio into the big leagues. Tony Lazzeri, and Frank Crosetti chaperoned the rookie. The two Italian-American veterans were, like DiMaggio, products of San Francisco with more in common with the new kid than Gehrig, the New York City product.

Gehrig's last full season was 1938, and by the end of it, the Yankees had won the second and third of four successive World Series championships. DiMaggio led the league in batting in '39 and '40, batting a career-high .381 and winning the first of his three Most Valuable Player awards in the

When Joe shared the benefit of his baseball knowledge, Yankees such as Mickey Mantle and Yogi Berra were all ears.

year that brought Gehrig's retirement.

The second MVP Award and another World Series ring came in 1941, DiMaggio's signature season. His stature and popularity were greater than ever.

The Yankees won again in 1943, DiMaggio's first year in the Army Air Forces, but they finished third and fourth without him in '44 and '45, unwittingly reinforcing his value. Decades before Paul Simon's song "Mrs. Robinson," the question was asked: "Where have you gone, Joe DiMaggio?" And not only in a baseball sense. DiMaggio was missed by housewives in California, grandfathers in Michigan and pre-teens in Alabama, not just merely by fathers in the Bronx.

His first season back from military duty brought another third-place finish. But beginning with 1947 and through his final season — and Mantle's first — in 1951, the Yankees won four World Series titles. The dynasty had extended into a fourth decade, and DiMaggio would hand off the torch to Mantle before the next season.

Gehrig, DiMaggio and Yankees catcher Bill Dickey enjoyed good times off the field as they were winning championships on it.

Their lives intersected more after DiMaggio's retirement than during the partial season they spent together as teammates in '51. Mantle held DiMaggio in awe. But little teacher-student interaction occurred between the two. DiMaggio had Crosetti and Lazzeri, Mantle had Whitey Ford and Billy Martin. And DiMaggio, always so reserved, wasn't one to initiate a relationship or even a conversation.

Not that it ever mattered to the masses. In 13 glorious seasons, DiMaggio had become as readily associated with success and positive qualities as he subsequently became identified with Mr. Coffee. He hadn't hit 60 or 714 home runs, hadn't played in 2,130 consecutive games, won a Triple Crown or launched home runs that defied gravity, logic and accurate measurement. But his place among the legendary Yankees was secured. From The Bambino, to The Iron Horse, to The Yankee

AP / WIDE WORLD PHOTOS

Clipper to The Magnificent 7. The Fab Four. No sports franchise ever has matched that sequence.

Each afforded the Yankees tradition a different texture and evoked different responses from the public. Ruth was enjoyed; Gehrig admired; Mantle, beloved. And DiMaggio, the son of an Italian immigrant fisherman, was respected. From San Francisco, where he became a baseball hero before reaching the big leagues, to the Bronx, where he brought the element of dignity to the field, he was, above all else, respected — everywhere by everyone.

Always the focus of the media's attention, Gehrig and DiMaggio, along with manager Joe McCarthy (left) and owner Jacob Ruppert, prepare to speak to reporters after winning the 1937 World Series.

Ruth was a smile, a wink, a hot dog and a home run. A beer, a belly and a bomb. He was the human fun house and the man who forged baseball's place in this country.

Gehrig was a symbol of perseverance and courage. And it didn't hurt that he could hit. His name became attached to the disease that killed him, an odd legacy, but one that indicated he'd transcended the game as Ruth had. Mantle was, at one time, invincible and vulnerable; powerful but betrayed by his body's weaknesses. The perfect idol for the first generation of television viewers.

DiMaggio was all of the above, but mostly he was respected. And the degree to which he earned that respect seemingly exceeded the degree to which he was genuinely liked. Not that many disliked him. But few people thought they knew him well. Even his teammates thought DiMaggio wouldn't let you look inside. It has been suggested that his pristine image exists at least partially because he hid his true self away. In his generation, privacy was more treasured and the media was less aggressive. The right to know wasn't exercised so much and rarely was abused.

On the field, he showed you everything — a combination of grace, speed, power, baseball acumen and a certain innate elegance that distinguished him from his colleagues and opponents. Some believe DiMaggio was the first player skilled in all facets of the game.

Though greatly reserved, he too exceeded the parameters of the field. He went beyond the ball. He was saluted in Simon's lyrics and his uniqueness was acknowledged in Hemingway's *The Old Man and the Sea*: "I would like to take the great DiMaggio fishing." It seemed that simple adjective, "great," became permanently affixed to his surname.

And, of course, he was an entry in the list of favorite things submitted by Virginia O'Neill-Houchin, a sentiment no doubt shared by so many citizens across the country.

Marty Noble covers Major League Baseball for Newsday.

Leading Man

Whether he was leading with his bat,
with encouraging words or by his mere presence,
Joe DiMaggio was a figure of admiration and
inspiration to his Yankees teammates

For all his magnificence, mysteriousness and understated elegance, Joseph Paul DiMaggio was simply an artisan on the diamond. He was a master at his craft, an athlete who brought a rare combination of talent to the right place at the right time. He, consequently, defined an era.

In San Francisco, his stature as a schoolboy and sandlot standout grew to such epic proportions that a bidding war for his services ensued an entire coast away. He would not disappoint his top bidders, the New York Yankees, the team with which he collected nine world championships during 13 seasons of service. Nor did he disappoint his many teammates along the way. They revered his abilities and quiet manner. Joe DiMaggio became the focal point for a generation of Yankees squads that would seasonally, methodically wreak havoc upon the American League.

His teammates, from Joe's rookie year in 1936 to his retirement in 1951, encountered a player possessing an unbridled passion for a sport he adored, and a man who played the game at a level they were not accustomed to. DiMaggio was neither fiery nor particularly verbal. But there was a spark, a commitment, a look that entranced his teammates into performing with a redefined sense of purpose.

By Gregg Mazzola

The Yankees could always count on Joe coming through in the clutch for them, as he did late in the 1948 season when his 10th-inning grand slam home run shocked the league-leading Red Sox.

During his 13 seasons as a Yankee, Joe helped carry his teammates to glory, and sometimes they returned the favor.

Mel Allen, the long time voice of the Yankees, saw in DiMaggio a man who could inspire by his presence alone and who over time accepted the role as team leader.

"I began to notice before games that Joe became the point man to his teammates," Allen says. "I don't think there was any planning to this. Just before the 'bell' would ring, the starters would be on the top steps of the dugout to take the field. When they started out onto the field, Joe was always the first one out and the other players would be a little behind him, almost like an inverted 'V.'

"I always had this feeling that in tight situations late in the game, I could see [shortstop Phil] Rizzuto look out to Joe and get a lift."

Allen's intuition was impeccable. Before long, Joe's stature began growing in legendary proportions as his streak of brilliant play continued. Teammates who performed wondrous deeds of their own were buoyed by the fact that Joe was on their side.

"He was like a security blanket," says Rizzuto, a teammate of Joe's for eight seasons. "During games with a lot of pressure, you could just turn around to make sure Joe was in center."

Not only was Joe in center, but he was always the center of attention, sometimes much to his chagrin. A simple walk down a Manhattan street caused a commotion that made him a prisoner of his own celebrity. In the clubhouse, though, Joe was not afraid to use his clout when he had to.

"[Yankees manager] Joe McCarthy liked to see if as a rookie you were man enough to handle a situation without going crying to the manager," Rizzuto explains. "When I came up to replace [Frankie] Crosetti, none of the veterans talked to me. I couldn't even take batting practice. Then Joe stepped in and told the veterans to let me hit. From that point on, everything was fine."

DiMaggio's teammates began to better understand the personality and nuances of their All-Star outfielder. He indeed was difficult to get close to. Most often, conversations with him revolved solely around baseball. They respected his privacy and instead gravitated toward his single-mindedness toward winning ball games.

"Being quiet was always his nature," says Tommy Henrich, DiMaggio's teammate from 1937 to 1942, and from 1946 to 1950. "That's the way he was all his life. That's the way he was made, and that's the way he stayed. I never tried to get to know him better. I respected the way he was.

"Joe D was the best winner I ever saw," Henrich adds. "It was very important to win that ball game. He wanted to participate as much as he could. To Joe, baseball was always the team first."

For all his greatness, DiMaggio was a man of humility, a man who despised drawing attention for his success. He was, in his eyes, simply a ballplayer. But to his teammates, he was a true champion.

"He was really an imperial type of player," says former Yankees second baseman Jerry Coleman. "He had the posture, the stance. He had such a magnificent carriage about him — like no one else I ever saw."

His poise was exceeded only by his work ethic and his enthusiasm for the game he loved.

"He ran out every single ball," Allen explains. "I remember so often on an ordinary single, he'd run around first base looking for the slightest bobble. Then he'd have to stop at top speed and pull up short. That to me exemplified what made him a champion.

"Whenever someone would mention a great play or something, Joe would say, 'I'm just an old pro.'

His teammates remember him as much more.

Gregg Mazzola is the editor of Yankees Magazine.

From the moment he arrived in New York, Joe (second from right) was an explosive offensive weapon on every Yankees team he played for.

Portrait of a Hero

Joe may have been a heroic figure to fans and teammates, but as the following pages suggest, there were many facets to his persona

The classic images of Joe DiMaggio have evolved throughout the years. From his days as a young star with the Yankees to his role as a distinguished alumnus at Yankees games and on to a starring appearance at old-timer's days at the Stadium, Joe DiMaggio's career is certainly worth a tip of the cap.

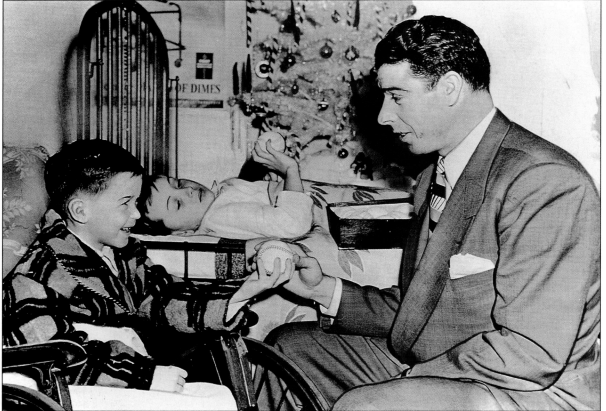

Joe's natural affinity for children began many years before he took on a lead role in founding the Joe DiMaggio Children's Hospital in Hollywood, Fla., in 1992. And all throughout his career, Joe's youngest fans may have been his most fervent ones.

Despite Joe's success on the baseball field and overwhelming popularity, his family remained a priority in his life. Whether it be during his parents' 50th wedding anniversary, a discussion with older brother Tom, a baseball reunion with brothers Vince and Dom or through the voice of a radio announcer during Yankees games, Joe remained connected to those who were most important to him.

What Might Have Been

At the peak of his abilities, Joe DiMaggio
sacrificed three seasons to serve his country during
World War II. What could he and the Yankees
have achieved had his career not been interrupted?

When World War II drained our National Pastime of its talent from 1942 to 1945, the careers of many professional baseball players were forever altered. During that three-year period, nearly 500 major leaguers and 3,500 minor league players joined 11 million other Americans in defending their country.

Players in their prime, honoring the colors of the flag, were deprived of as many as three valuable years in a pursuit that offered few guarantees.

Yankees superstar Joe DiMaggio was no exception to the rule, although his marital status kept him on the playing field during the war's initial unfolding.

So when the Yankee Clipper took on his wartime obligation in 1943, he left behind two Most Valuable Player awards, five World Series rings, two batting titles and a reputation as the game's most complete player.

DiMaggio was just 28 when he was assigned to Special Services and stationed at the Santa Ana Air Base in California. One can only imagine how his absence from the diamond ultimately affected his place on baseball's all-time records lists. Or how it affected the Yankees themselves, who managed to win the World Series in '43 without him, but slipped among the mortals

By Gregg Mazzola

Although Joe connected on 361 career home runs, he most certainly would have surpassed the 400-homer mark had his career not been interrupted by the war.

the ensuing two sea-sons.

DiMaggio returned to Yankee pinstripes at the age of 31, clearly beyond his prime as an athlete. While the slugger spent most of wartime playing ball for several outfits of the armed forces — as did most major lea-guers — the competi-tion was a far cry from what he was accustomed to.

In addition, upon Joe's return, many of his former teammates such as Red Rolfe, George Selkirk, Bill Dickey, Frank Crosetti and Lefty Gomez either had retired or had seen their playing skills deteriorate. Joe himself was 10-15 pounds lighter and was in poor health, the result of an ulcer many believed was abetted by marital difficulties.

The 1944 and '45 Yankees clearly exhibited their need for a healthy DiMaggio in the lineup and in the clubhouse. The club finished in third and fourth place. Joe's leadership was sorely missed. Baseball and its fans alike were ecstatic at seeing the stars of the game return in 1946. But the time away from the game took its toll on players' skills, and Joe was no exception.

Yankees fans who once marveled at the gallantry of their wunderkind in center field were in for a rude awakening upon Joe's return. While Yankee Stadium's turnstiles clicked at a record pace, DiMaggio suffered through a sub-par campaign, hitting a disappointing .290, yet managing 25 homers in a park that at times completely frustrated him.

Playing in Yankee Stadium was frustrating for righthanded power hitters because of an imposing outfield alignment that reached as deep as 461 feet in center field.

Says Mel Allen, longtime voice of the Yankees: "One thing that would tear Joe's heart out was hitting in Yankee Stadium and losing a lot of home runs because of the dimensions.

"He'd hit 400-plus foot drives that would not be home runs. I bet he would have hit another 150 homers in another park."

DiMaggio's 361 lifetime homers still stand just fourth-best on the Yankees' all-time list, 132 behind Lou Gehrig (who played four more sea-sons than Joe) and a healthy 298 in back of The Bambino, Babe Ruth, who heads the team's list.

And what about a hitter's all-time greatest goal of 3,000 hits? With his career total of 2,214 hits, DiMaggio would have needed to average 262 hits in each of the three seasons he missed — practically an impossible task even for the greatest of hitters. However, a realistic goal of 169 hits per season would have placed DiMaggio atop the Yankees' all-time career hits list, where he would have remained today.

Compounding the situation, the '46 Yankees finished 20 games above .500, but a whopping 17 games behind first-place Boston. Whispers that DiMaggio was at the crossroads of his career arose and were evident in the off-season when Yankees general manager Larry MacPhail offered his All-Star center fielder in a straight-up deal for Washington Senators hitting machine Mickey Vernon. Fortunately for the Yankees, and MacPhail, the deal was never consummated.

A postwar phenomena was growing for the maturing DiMaggio. In four of his final five seasons, Joltin' Joe led his troops not only to the postseason, but to world championships.

This newfound compassion for DiMaggio's skills was never more evident than in the '47 season. Joe hit just .315 with 20 homers and 97 RBI, yet earned the league's MVP Award as the Yankees captured another world title. He again was perceived as the indomitable piece to the Yankees' puzzle. Ted Williams' statistics in 1947 glistened mightily compared to DiMaggio's, but the perception endured that the Yankee Clipper still was the consummate team player. As Williams was making a name for himself in the record books, DiMaggio was collecting World Series rings.

Age was slowly creeping up on Joe, as were injuries that limited his playing time. From 1946 to 1951, DiMaggio never played a full 154-game season as heel spurs and assorted ailments took their toll. But as one writer said about Joe, "As DiMaggio goes, so goes the Yankees."

It is unlikely DiMaggio's involvement in the war affected his place among baseball's all-time record-setters. He played too few games and too few seasons.

War or no war, Joe DiMaggio played not for the records or for the glory. He played for the team. So in 1951, when the rigors of a 13th and final season had passed, the great one said goodbye to a team and a tradition, with dignity. And without remorse.

Gregg Mazzola is the editor of Yankees Magazine.

Had DiMaggio not spent three seasons in the Army Air Forces, he might have sewn up even more MVP awards and World Series titles with the Yankees.

ARCHIVE PHOTOS

Still at Full Sail

Well into his fourth decade of retirement, the Yankee Clipper continues to chart a distinctive course through the American consciousness

On that historic evening in Baltimore, Sept. 6, 1995, Orioles shortstop Cal Ripken Jr. played in consecutive game No. 2,131, surpassing the record of the legendary Lou Gehrig.

The love-in began.

Balloons were unfurled. Banners sprung up everywhere in Oriole Park at Camden Yards. The standing ovation continued endlessly. Ripken hugged about a hundred people during the celebration.

Joe DiMaggio sat quietly upstairs in the private box of Orioles owner Peter Angelos. DiMaggio later congratulated Ripken in person during postgame ceremonies.

It seems that's the way it's been with Joe DiMaggio for about 45 years. For a major baseball event to be official, historic and romantic, the great DiMaggio must be a part of the scene.

As a teammate of Gehrig with the Yankees from 1936 through Gehrig's retirement on July 4, 1939, DiMaggio represented the perfect living link for this special occasion.

In the summer of 1969, as baseball celebrated its centennial, DiMaggio, some 18 years after his retirement, was named the game's Greatest Living Player.

By Maury Allen

Even decades after retiring from baseball, Joe still maintained that picture-perfect form when delivering a throw.

DiMaggio was the glowing star among a collection of past and present heroes who toured the White House with President Nixon during their stay in Washington for the All-Star Game weekend.

DiMaggio's hold on the public psyche, on baseball fans in general and on America's insatiable appetite for heroic figures has been unmatched. No man has represented the game with more honor and glory for nearly half a century than DiMaggio.

DiMaggio played just 13 seasons. Many played longer and have better statistics. He does not lead in home runs, RBI, hits or consecutive games played.

He does lead, almost without argument, in the affection and respect of millions of Americans, many of whom never saw him play. After all, it's been 60 years since he first suited up for the Yankees in 1936, and almost 45 years since his retirement.

About a quarter of a century after he retired, I wrote a book about him titled, *Where Have You Gone, Joe DiMaggio?* a title borrowed from Paul Simon's classic line from "Mrs. Robinson," in the film *The Graduate*.

As a New York sportswriter, I knew where he went. He was at Yankees old-timers games. He was on the field as an Oakland Athletics coach

Although Joe did his slugging with his bat, not his fists, he still fit in with another sports icon of that era, heavyweight boxing champ Rocky Marciano during a visit with President Eisenhower at the White House in 1953.

wearing team owner Charlie Finley's garish green-and-white uniforms. He was at the Yankees' spring training. He was at charity golf tournaments, baseball card shows and in advertising offices going over his lines for Mr. Coffee and the Bowery Savings Bank commercials.

What I didn't know was why his career ended so early, at the age of 36, when veteran players generally hang on for a few more paychecks. His decision to retire following the '51 season intrigued me.

I traveled to San Francisco and met with his brother, Tom, who ran the famous family restaurant, DiMaggio's, on Fisherman's Wharf.

I wanted to know if Joe had told family members why he walked away from the Yankees even though general manager George Weiss offered him another $100,000, a princely sum in the early 1950s.

"Don't you know?" Tom DiMaggio asked. "He wasn't Joe DiMaggio anymore."

Finally, I understood.

DiMaggio had standards few players, and few Americans, could relate to. He knew what he meant to America. He understood his role, his image, his significance on the American scene. He would not tarnish it with play beneath his own standard.

The late Edward Bennett Williams, a famed attorney and friend of DiMaggio's, once was asked about Joe's intensity even in his final days as a player.

"Joe once told me that he played every game as hard as he could because he realized each day some youngster was seeing him for the first time," Williams said. "He would not disappoint them."

As Yankees fans often found out during old-timers games, Joe hadn't lost a step when it came to playing center field.

DiMaggio's first job after retirement was as a commentator on the Yankees' postgame television show. Public relations man Jackie Farrell had arranged it.

"There wasn't much to it," Farrell says. "Joe just had to make the opening greeting, and the pro announcers really took it from there. For hours Joe rehearsed the opening, 'Hi, I'm Joe DiMaggio.' He kept doing that over and over until it sounded right to him."

If there is one aspect of DiMaggio's retirement years that remains part of his character, it is his unfaltering sense of integrity. He maintains his connections only with events of dignity.

Probably his most stylish connection lies with the Joe DiMaggio Children's Hospital in Hollywood, Fla., which he now represents and raises funds for with almost every appearance he makes. If a promoter wants Joe DiMaggio at a golf tournament, often the cost is a significant contribution to the hospital.

Hundreds of children live better lives now because of Joe's dedication and generosity.

DiMaggio's role in American folklore probably began during his 56-game hitting streak in 1941. Les Brown and his orchestra introduced a song that summer written by Alan Courtney and Ben Homer, titled "Joltin' Joe DiMaggio."

He'll live in Baseball's Hall of Fame,
He got there blow by blow.
Our kids will tell their kids his name,
Joltin' Joe DiMaggio.

They still do tell their kids his name.

In that summer of 1941, DiMaggio attended the Joe Louis-Billy Conn boxing match with New York restaurateur Toots Shor and famed novelist Ernest Hemingway.

As the trio walked down the aisle toward their seats fans chanted, "Joe,

RALPH MORSE / LIFE MAGAZINE

Joe, Joe." One youngster managed to make eye contact with the bearded novelist.

"Hey," he asked, "are you anybody?"

"Yeah," Hemingway said, "I'm his doctor."

In Hemingway's Pulitzer Prize-winning novel, *The Old Man and the Sea*, the old fisherman showed his admiration for the Yankees outfielder.

"I wonder how the great DiMaggio would have liked the way I hit him in the brain," the old fisherman thought. "It was no great thing. Any man could do it. But do you think my hands were as great a handicap as the bone spurs?"

Later the fisherman would say, "You were born to be a fisherman as the fish was born to be a fish. San Pedro was a fisherman as was the father of the great DiMaggio."

Again, DiMaggio's name would surface in society as the standard of excellence — excellence he deemed he no longer possessed when he retired in 1951.

The brilliant musical play *South Pacific*, which opened in 1949, brought reference to DiMaggio's greatness.

"Bloody Mary is the girl I love," wrote Richard Rodgers and Oscar Hammerstein, "Bloody Mary is the girl I love. Her skin is as tender as DiMaggio's glove."

Not only did baseball come naturally to Joe, so did a concern for children as well, as evidenced by the establishment of the Joe DiMaggio Children's Hospital in Hollywood, Fla.

DiMaggio always has maintained a certain mystique about him, one of the reasons he remains an untarnished hero more than 45 years after he quit the game. He has no public feuds. He has never been involved in a public brawl. He has never criticized anyone publicly nor has he been criticized on the record.

Not even his brief marriage to Marilyn Monroe seemed to tarnish his image. He's never spoken publicly of her and has a habit of cutting off any friend who might choose to do so.

There is an award given annually by the New York Baseball Writers Association called the "Joe DiMaggio Toast of the Town" Award.

It was first presented in 1983, and since has been given to luminaries such as Willie Mays, Duke Snider and Mickey Mantle, players who performed at the highest level of the game and who had the most significant impact on baseball.

DiMaggio presented the inaugural award to a New York favorite then, Yankees outfielder Lou Piniella.

He arrived late at the New York Sheraton hotel, where the January dinner was held. He walked slowly through the doors toward the dais. The sound began first with a murmur of recognition, then some applause, followed by cries of "Joe, Joe, Joe," ringing out among 1,500 people.

As he approached the dais, the standing ovation rocked the room. DiMaggio stood there with a small smile.

Most in the room had never seen the grace of his play on the field. They could only revere the greatness of the man.

Maury Allen covered the Yankees for the New York Post.

As a former team- mate of Lou Gehrig, DiMaggio was the perfect link to Cal Ripken Jr. when the Orioles' Iron Man broke Gehrig's consecutive games played record in 1995.

He's No Average Joe

Befitting his stature as one of baseball's icons,
Joe DiMaggio boasts memorabilia
that's among the most treasured in the hobby

His image has become larger than life for people of all ages.

He made a name for himself in baseball during a time when television broadcasts from America's ballparks were a dream of the future. Just a select few personally witnessed him building an image of greatness.

So why does Joe DiMaggio remain so popular among so many Americans, reflected in the still-voracious appetite for his memorabilia, more than 45 years after his retirement?

From the sandlots of San Francisco to the hallowed Yankee Stadium, Joe DiMaggio lived the American dream. Many baseball fans lived out their own similar dreams through DiMaggio's actions, not only on the field, but off it as well. Joe was the consummate player and gentleman.

In leading the New York Yankees to nine World Series championships in his 13 seasons with the team, Joe DiMaggio became a hero to many and a living legend to others.

As he's come to occupy a special place in American lore, it seems as if everyone wants a part of him. And because Americans do not have access to the man him-

By Mike Pagel

Baseballs with DiMaggio's signature command a three-figure premium.

self, they accept the next best thing: Joe DiMaggio memorabilia.

From his early days as a minor league outfielder with the San Francisco Seals, to his days as a spokesman for Bowery Savings Bank and Mr. Coffee, DiMaggio always has been in high demand. From bats, balls and jerseys to menus, glasses and match covers from his restaurant in San Francisco, interest remains high in any item associated with Joe.

Because DiMaggio's time with the San Francisco Seals coincided with the depths of the Great Depression, memorabilia from this period is difficult to locate. Of course, Pacific Coast League programs featuring the Seals include his name in the lineup. Most Depression programs were four-page scorecards, but they do turn up with some regularity and remain in heavy demand.

DiMaggio's first baseball card is a Zeenut issue, produced in 1934. Zeenuts are black-and-white cards that were inserted into confectionery

Joe had a tendency to draw a crowd any time he had a pen in hand and was willing to sign.

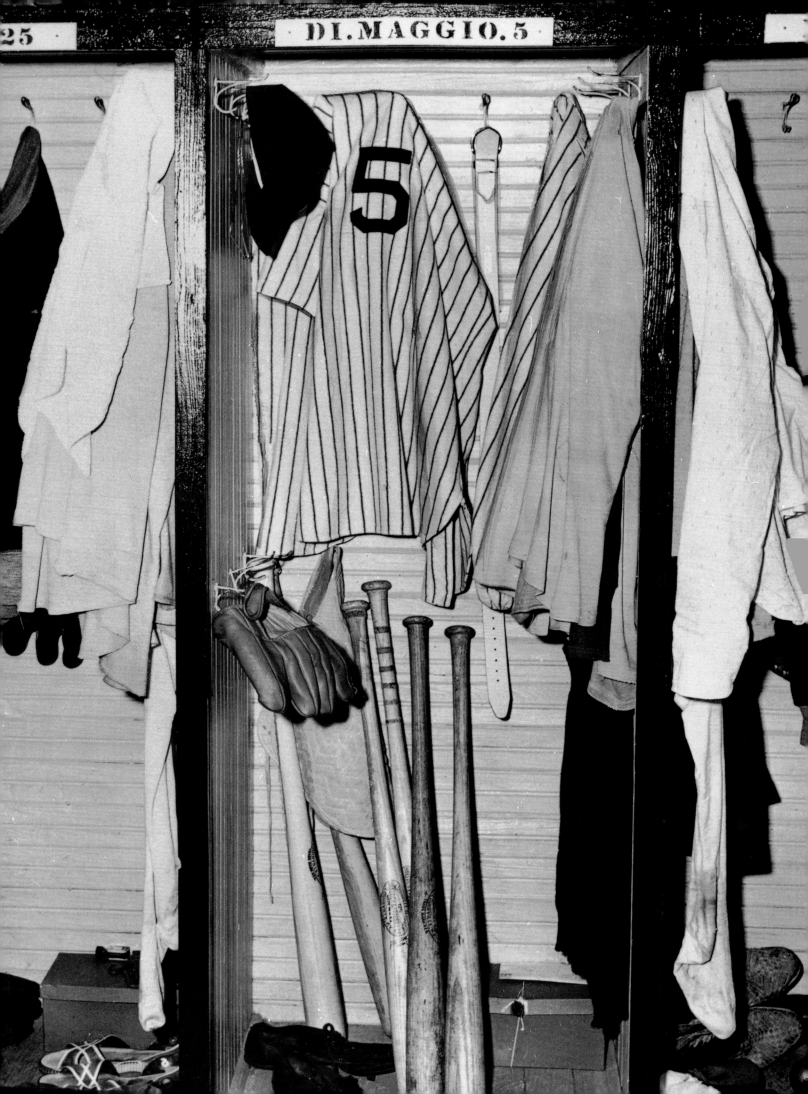

products sold on the West Coast. Names on the Zeenut cards of the three DiMaggio brothers all are spelled "DeMaggio," and because kids used to play card games similar to pitching pennies, Mint Zeenuts are scarce. A Joe "DeMaggio" card in Near-Mint or better condition commands a four-figure premium.

A second "DeMaggio" Zeenut was issued in 1935, and is in equal demand as the first. But there is another DiMaggio card from 1935, and it is scarce beyond belief. San Francisco radio station KYA unveiled a promotion in which fans could send in a penny postcard each week and in return receive a postcard featuring a member of either the Seals, the Oakland Oaks or the San Francisco Missions baseball clubs. There are seven known versions of baseball player cards that were mailed out.

Each card had a notation next to the player's name, "Compliments of Pebble Beach," a local clothing producer. Each card was personally signed by the player. Joe's autograph read "J. DiMaggio," noting the correct spelling of his last name along with only his first initial. The abbreviated autograph seemed to be the norm for Joe during his Seals years. Scarce as they are, Pebble Beach cards in Mint or Near-Mint condition change hands for as much as $5,000.

Photos of Joe as a Seal have proven to be relatively common. Because he was so popular in the PCL, an abundance of photos were taken. Many have been reproduced for signing sessions. Most of these reproduced photos were signed with a Sharpie pen. Autographed photos of Joe during his San Francisco Seals days sell for about $100.

While equipment from that era is hard to find, a few DiMaggio bats from his Seals days reportedly have survived. These are in heavy demand and generally require a substantial premium of as much as $20,000 each, depending on their condition.

DiMaggio's family operated restaurant, which closed in 1986 after nearly 50 years of business, brought to the market some interesting memorabilia.

Items such as match covers, napkins, menus and water glasses from the San Francisco restaurant exist but are not easily found.

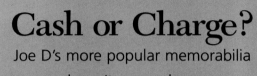

Cash or Charge?

Joe D's more popular memorabilia doesn't come cheap

New York Yankees:
- Game-worn jersey — $200,000
- Game-used bat — $22,000
- Game-worn cap — $18,000
- September '46 issue of *Sport* — $250

San Francisco Seals:
- Joe DiMaggio Pebble Beach card — $5,000
- Autographed photo — $100
- Game-used bat — $20,000

DiMaggio's restaurant:
- Match cover — $40
- Napkin — $25
- Menu — $150
- Autographed menu — $300
- Water glass — $100
- Pennant — $500

DiMaggio's restaurant in San Francisco remained a popular attraction for nearly 50 years before closing in 1986.

As many as 15 different versions of the match covers exist and sell for as much as $40 each. DiMaggio's napkins, perhaps the most available restaurant item, can be obtained for about $25 each. And a vintage DiMaggio's menu, which is one of the most difficult of these items to locate, sells in the $300 range with Joe's signature and $150 without.

DiMaggio's restaurant stopped using the famed water glasses in the mid-1970s because many customers continually stole the glasses as they left the premises. The small glass features a rendition of Joe swinging a bat, etched in blue. The script on the glass also is blue and simply reads: "DiMaggio's." Today, the glasses are valued at about $100 each.

Swizzle sticks, sugar packets and postcards also remain as souvenirs from the restaurant. These are considered less significant items and can be obtained for a much smaller fee. Most postcards sell for $25-$35. But the most popular postcard, which is made of linen and features the three DiMaggio baseball brothers, sells for up to $50. Pennants and ashtrays also are available as souvenirs from the DiMaggio restaurant. They have been known to sell in the $500 price range.

DiMaggio's most popular memorabilia continues to be items from his glorious Yankees days.

DiMaggio's game-worn Yankees jerseys have ranged in price from $50,000 to $200,000 each, while a game-used, autographed bat recently commanded a $22,000 premium. Also, DiMaggio's game-used Yankees caps have been known to sell for as much as $18,000 in the last several years.

Other DiMaggio memorabilia from his days as a Yankee include autographed balls, model gloves, cards, buttons and pins. Joe autographed

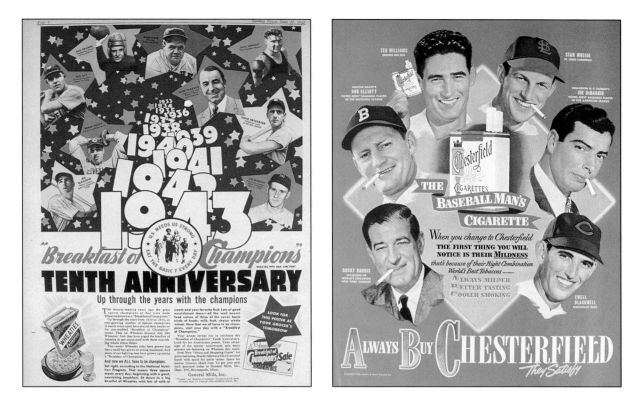

Joltin' Joe promoted everything from Chesterfield smokes to Avon products during his playing career. Now vintage collectors come calling for copies of DiMaggio's earlier ads.

Supply and DiMand

The demand for Joe DiMaggio cards far exceeds the limited supply the market has to offer

1938 Goudey Heads Up #274

Looking for Joe DiMaggio cards? Haven't had much luck finding any? There's a simple explanation for that. The number of cards Joe DiMaggio appears on is quite limited.

DiMaggio played baseball in an era when cards were not mass-produced as they are today. In fact, during World War II and through 1947, hardly any cards were produced at all. When Bowman and Topps, the two card manufacturers at the time, resumed production of cards, DiMaggio didn't sign a contract with either one and therefore wasn't included in their major sets. In 1951, Joe retired from the game, and soon thereafter card companies discontinued their pursuit of him.

However, DiMaggio appears on several pre-war vintage issues such as 1939 Play Ball #92, 1940 Play Ball #1, 1941 Play Ball #71 and 1941 Double Play #63. These popular issues range in value from $750 for the '41 Double Play card to $3,000 for the '40 Play Ball card. DiMaggio's 1938 Goudey Heads Up #274 issue, which is valued at $5,000, has become one of his most prominent Yankees cards.

In the '50s, Joe was featured on several oddball issues such as 1952 Berk Ross #13, which sells for $1,250 in Mint condition.

Nearly a decade later, the Nu-Card Company produced two newspaper style card sets that feature cards of the Yankee Clipper. Those most notable include his 1960 Nu-Card Hi-Lites #38 and his 1961 Nu-Card Scoops #438. Both cards carry the theme of DiMaggio's 56-game hitting streak and sell in the more affordable range of $15-$25.

In 1992, Score honored DiMaggio with a five-card insert set. Joe autographed 2,500 of these cards, 2,495 of which were randomly inserted into Series I packs. The other five were given away through a mail-in sweepstakes. The autographed issue sells for as much as $600, while the regular inserts sell for about $40 each.

1993 Pinnacle DiMaggio Set #25

Three additional DiMaggio cards were included in the 1992 Score Factory Inserts set. Although their value is between 60 cents and $1.50, these cards generally are not as available as singles since few dealers are willing to break the set.

One year later, Pinnacle capitalized on Joe's renewed popularity by producing a 30-card set commemorating his life and career. DiMaggio signed 9,000 cards that were randomly inserted into the 209,000 sets produced.

1992 Score Factory Insert #B12

And in 1995, Old Judge included Joe DiMaggio in its 36-card set (#JD1). DiMaggio signed 250 issues for insertion into the Old Judge Signatures set. The autographed cards list for as much as $400.

So you see, there are DiMaggio cards in circulation. Sure, locating and obtaining the cards may not be an easy task, but for the devoted DiMaggio collector, it certainly is a rewarding one.   — Mike Pagel

Joe DiMaggio autographed bats have been among the Yankee Clipper's most popular memorabilia items.

balls are quite abundant and can be obtained for as little as $140.

Hundreds of magazine covers also exist for DiMaggio memorabilia collectors. The most popular DiMaggio magazine cover is the first issue of *Sport*, which hit newsstands in September 1946. The magazine, which features Joe holding his young son on his lap, sells for about $250 in good condition. Joe also appeared on *Sport* magazine covers in each of the next three years.

DiMaggio also graces the cover of a number of non-sports magazines such as *Life, Time* and *Look*. The magazine covers present the most feasible option for collectors looking for DiMaggio memorabilia from his Yankees years. They are somewhat easier to locate and won't cost collectors an arm and a leg.

Collectors can expect to pay a hefty price for a DiMaggio-worn jersey.

In October 1991, Scoreboard signed Joe to an exclusive two-year contract to sign balls and photos. During that time, DiMaggio honored his relationship with Scoreboard by not signing any other baseballs. The demand and the price for a DiMaggio-signed ball skyrocketed. Scoreboard retailed the autographed balls at $390 but reduced the price to as low as $249 because of a low number of sales at the original price.

Ken Goldin, president and CEO at Scoreboard, says the autographed balls are sold out and the photo inventory has been significantly reduced as well.

Obtaining DiMaggio's autograph in person can be a difficult task because of Joe's low profile. Joe, who turned 80 in 1994, rarely makes a public appearance primarily because of health concerns. DiMaggio occasionally will sign at a show, but his high appearance fee tends to discourage promoters from seeking him. It has been reported that DiMaggio commands $100,000 for an appearance, which leads promoters to charge no less than $150 for his autograph.

DiMaggio's exceptional demands in the hobby industry can be justified in part due to

Joe DiMaggio

Comprehensive Card Checklist & Price Guide

- ❏ 1937 Exh 4-in-1 #13 Multiplayer . . . $600-$1,100
- ❏ 1937 OPC #118 . . . . $2,400-$4,000
- ❏ 1937 Wheaties BB7 #29I . . . . $250-$400
- ❏ 1938 Exhibit 4-on-1 #13 . . . . $700-$1,200
- ❏ 1938 Goudey Heads Up #250 . . . . $2,500-$5,000
- ❏ 1938 Goudey Heads Up #274 . . . . $2,500-$5,000
- ❏ 1938 ONG/Pin-#7. . . . . $75-$125
- ❏ 1938 Wheaties BB15 #2. . . . . $300-$500
- ❏ 1939 Exhibit #13 . . . . $30-$50
- ❏ 1939 Play Ball #26 . . . . $1,250-$2,500
- ❏ 1940 Play Ball #1 . . . . $1,500-$3,000
- ❏ 1940 Wheaties M4 #2A
  Multiplayer. $125-$200
- ❏ 1940 Wheaties M4 #2B
  Multiplayer. $125-$200
- ❏ 1941 Double Play #63 . . . . $400-$750
- ❏ 1941 Play Ball #71 . . . . $1,500-$2,750
- ❏ 1941 Wheaties M5 #17
  Multiplayer. $125-$200
- ❏ 1947 Homogenized Bond #10. . . . . . $150-$250
- ❏ 1949 Leaf #1 . . . . $2,100-$3,200
- ❏ 1948 Swell #15 . . . . $30-$60
- ❏ 1950 W576 Callahan #27. . . . . $90-$150
- ❏ 1951 Berk Ross #B5 . . . . $100-$175
- ❏ 1952 Berk Ross #13. . . . . $650-$1,250
- ❏ 1953 Canadian Exhibit #28 . . . . $125-$200
- ❏ 1960 Nu-Card Highlights #7 . . . . $15-$25
- ❏ 1960 Nu-Card Highlights #38 . . . . $15-$25
- ❏ 1961 Golden Press #9 . . . . $20-$35
- ❏ 1961 Nu-Card Scoops #438 . . . . $9-$15
- ❏ 1961 Nu-Card Scoops #467 . . . . $9-$15
- ❏ 1963 Gad Fun Cards #33 . . . . $25-$50
- ❏ 1969 A's Jack In The Box #5 Coach . . . . . $40-$75
- ❏ 1972 Laughlin Great Feats #1 . . . . $2-$4
- ❏ 1973 Syracuse Team #7 . . . . $45-$75
- ❏ 1974 Laughlin All Star Game #39. . . . . $1.50-$3
- ❏ 1974 Syracuse Team #5 . . . . $45-$75
- ❏ 1975 Shakey's #1. . . . . $10-$20
- ❏ 1976 Laughlin Jubilee #25 . . . . $2.50-$5
- ❏ 1975 42 Play Ball #2 . . . . $5-$10
- ❏ 1976 Rowe #4 . . . . $10-$20
- ❏ 1976 Shakey's #74 . . . . $10-$20
- ❏ 1977 Galasso #1. . . . . $1.50-$3
- ❏ 1977 Galasso #235 . . . . $1.50-$3
- ❏ 1977 Shakey's #24 . . . . $10-$20
- ❏ 1979 TCMA Stars of the 50s #1. . . . . $5-$10
- ❏ 1980 Marchant/HOF #10. . . . . $3-$5
- ❏ 1980 Pacific Legends #5 . . . . $3-$5
- ❏ 1980 Perez Steele HOF #75 . . . . $30-$50

- ❏ 1980 SSPC HOF . . . . $1-$2
- ❏ 1983 TCMA Yankee Yearbook
  Insert Sheet #1 . . . . $3-$5
- ❏ 1984 West #1-5. . . . . $1-$2 each
- ❏ 1985 Sportflics Prototype #1 . . . . $60-$100
- ❏ 1986 Sportflics Decade Greats #20 . . . . . . $2-$3
- ❏ 1988 Pacific Legends #100 . . . . $2-$4
- ❏ 1989 HOF Stickers #39 . . . . $1-$2
- ❏ 1989 Kenner Starting Lineup
  Baseball Greats #5 Multiplayer. . . . . $35-$65
- ❏ 1990 Baseball Wit #49 . . . . $.50-$1
- ❏ 1990 HOF Stickers #39 . . . . $.50-$1
- ❏ 1992 Score DiMaggio Set . . . . $100-$200
- ❏ 1992 Score DiMaggio Autograph . . . . $400-$550
- ❏ 1992 Score Factory Inserts #B12 . . . . $.60-$1.50
- ❏ 1992 Score Factory Inserts #B13 . . . . $.60-$1.50
- ❏ 1992 Score Factory Inserts #B14 . . . . $.60-$1.50
- ❏ 1992 Yankee WIZ AS #18 . . . . $2-$4
- ❏ 1992 Yankee WIZ HOF #9 . . . . $1.50-$3
- ❏ 1993 Pinnacle DiMaggio Set . . . . $12-$22
- ❏ 1993 Pinnacle DiMaggio
  Autographed Set . . . . $900-$1,500
- ❏ 1995 Signature Rookies
  Old Judge #JD1 . . . . $4-$8
- ❏ 1995 Signature Rookies Old Judge
  T-$95 #JD1 Autographed . . . . $275-$400
- ❏ PM10 #39 . . . . $100-$175
- ❏ PM10 #40 . . . . $100-$175
- ❏ PM10 #41A . . . . $25-$40
- ❏ PM10 #41B . . . . $100-$175
- ❏ PM10 #42 . . . . $100-$175
- ❏ PM10 #43 . . . . $150-$250
- ❏ PR1 #7 . . . . $250-$400
- ❏ R302-1 #9 . . . . $50-$80
- ❏ R302-2 #105 . . . . $50-$80
- ❏ R303A #13 . . . . $250-$400
- ❏ R303B #6 . . . . $175-$300
- ❏ R311 Leather #L12 Multiplayer. . . . . . $150-$250
- ❏ R312 #A9 . . . . $200-$350
- ❏ R314 #A117 Multiplayer . . . . $75-$125
- ❏ R314 #C6 . . . . $150-$250
- ❏ R326-#4A . . . . $150-$250
- ❏ R326-#4B . . . . $150-$250
- ❏ R342-#4 . . . . $300-$500
- ❏ R346-#16 . . . . $175-$300
- ❏ R423-#25 . . . . $15-$30
- ❏ V300 #118 . . . . $2,400-$4,000
- ❏ V351A #11 . . . . $600-$1,000
- ❏ V351B #13 . . . . $150-$250
- ❏ V355 #51 . . . . $2,400-$4,000

1941 Play Ball #71

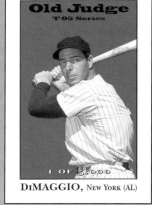

1995 Signature Rookies Old Judge #JD1

1977 Galasso #1

his direct contributions to the Joe DiMaggio Children's Hospital in Hollywood, Fla. Much of the hospital's expenses are funded by DiMaggio himself. The hospital accepts all children in need of medical treatment, whether or not their families can afford it.

At one of DiMaggio's more recent card show appearances — The 16th Long Island Classic in New York in '95 — DiMaggio signed 1,300 autographs and graciously allowed all customers the opportunity to have their picture taken with him. The price range for Joe's autograph at the show was $150 for baseballs, $175 for flat items, and $350 for caps and helmets. Joe also provided autographs at another show in '96 at Hofstra University in Uniondale, N.Y.

There are some items that DiMaggio generally does not sign. Like other big-name sports celebrities, Joe refuses to sign bats, jerseys, original art, statues and photo balls. Nor will he autograph any Mr. Coffee memorabilia or Marilyn Monroe memorabilia.

Obtaining DiMaggio autographed memorabilia has never been an easy task for collectors. And because in recent years DiMaggio has become more restrictive in his signing tendencies, his memorabilia should become less available and certainly more valuable.

Mike Pagel is an associate editor at Beckett Publications. Dick Dobbins, a Bay Area baseball historian and collector, also contributed to this story.

Never considered a prolific signer, DiMaggio is tough to catch with a pen in his hand.

Beckett Remembers

When Joe DiMaggio was elegantly stroking hits and winning championships with the Yankees in the 1930s and '40s, baseball card manufacturing was barely in its infancy. And even though the great Yankee Clipper had been retired from the game for more than three decades before we launched our inaugural issue of *Beckett Monthly*, Joe has not been overlooked. Whenever Joltin' Joe has graced the pages of *Beckett Baseball Card Monthly*, the issues have become especially memorable ones.

The article was called "A Final Look," but it was anything but. In this first-person narrative (December 1990, issue #69), Randy Cummings recounts an interview of a lifetime.

Artist Jerry Hersh paid tribute to legendary baseball players who have worn the hallowed Yankee pinstripes throughout the years. And Joe's image, in the middle of it all, stands out as a worthy focal point of the piece (August 1987, issue #30).

The 1941 season remains a special one, not just for two particular players, but for baseball, as well. "Joe & Ted's Excellent Season" (October 1991, issue #79) chronicles the phenomenal seasons Ted Williams and Joe DiMaggio compiled on the brink of another world war.

In one of the most awe-inspiring covers in *Beckett Baseball Card Monthly's* history, Joe appears with Gehrig, Ruth and Mantle in Yankee Fantasy, an original rendition by Bart Forbes displaying the founding fathers of the Yankee tradition (June 1991, issue #75).

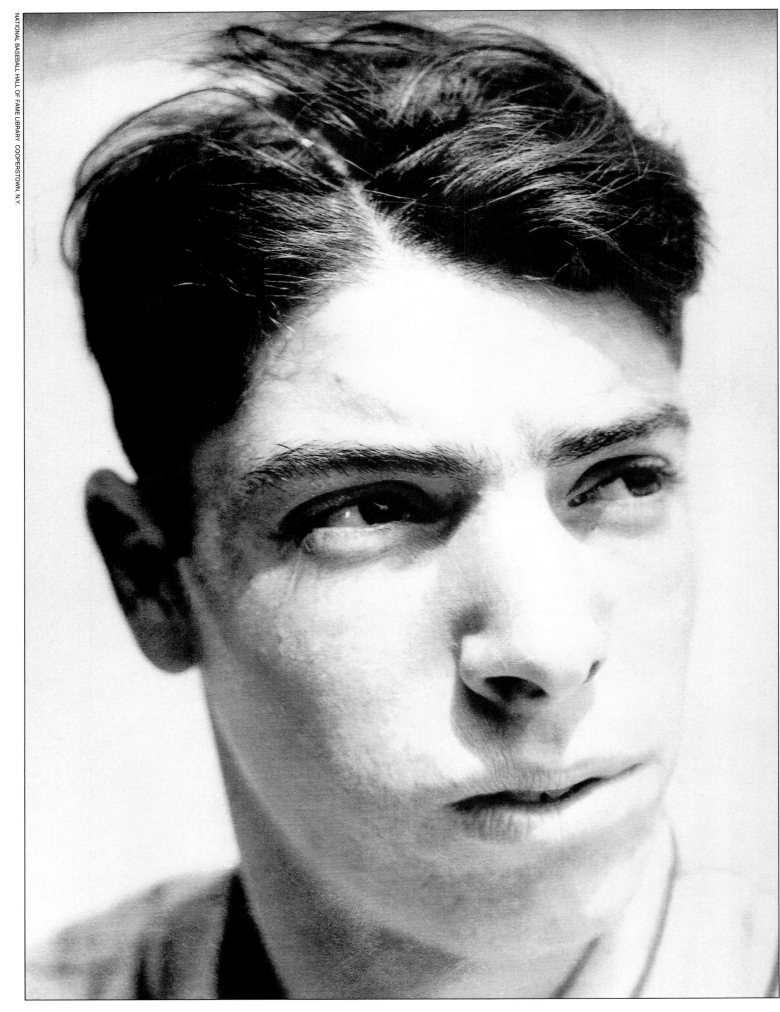